Silent Hill

LANDMARK VIDEO GAMES

The Landmark Video Games book series is the first in the English language in which each book addresses a specific video game or video game series in depth, examining it in the light of a variety of approaches, including game design, genre, form, content, meanings, and its context within video game history. The specific games or game series chosen are historically significant and influential games recognized not only for their quality of gameplay but also for setting new standards, introducing new ideas, incorporating new technology, or otherwise changing the course of a genre or area of video game history. The Landmark Video Games book series hopes to provide an intimate and detailed look at the history of video games through a study of exemplars that have paved the way and set the course that others would follow or emulate, and that became an important part of popular culture.

Myst *and* Riven: *The World of the D'ni*
by Mark J. P. Wolf

Silent Hill: *The Terror Engine*
by Bernard Perron

DIGITALCULTUREBOOKS, an imprint of the University of Michigan Press, is dedicated to publishing work in new media studies and the emerging field of digital humanities.

Silent Hill
The Terror Engine

Bernard Perron

The University of Michigan Press · *Ann Arbor*

Copyright © by Bernard Perron 2012
Some rights reserved

cc creative commons

This work is licensed under the Creative Commons Attribution-Noncommercial-No Derivative Works 3.0 United States License. To view a copy of this license, visit http://creativecommons.org/licenses/by-nc-nd/3.0/ or send a letter to Creative Commons, 171 Second Street, Suite 300, San Francisco, California, 94105, USA.

Published in the United States of America by
The University of Michigan Press
Manufactured in the United States of America
♾ Printed on acid-free paper

2015   2014   2013   2012   4   3   2   1

A CIP catalog record for this book is available from the British Library.

Library of Congress Cataloging-in-Publication Data

Perron, Bernard.
    Silent hill : the terror engine / Bernard Perron.
      p. cm. — (Landmark video games)
    Includes bibliographical references and index.
    ISBN 978-0-472-07162-3 (cloth : alk. paper) — ISBN 978-0-472-05162-5 (pbk. : alk. paper) — ISBN 978-0-472-02783-5 (e-book)
    1. Silent Hill (Game) I. Title.
GV1469.35.S54P47 2011
794.8—dc23   2011028327

Acknowledgments

I would like to thank:

Shantal Robert and Léa Elisabeth Perron who let me spend sleepless nights in Silent Hill throughout the years;

My parents, as always;

Matteo Bitanti and Costa Nolan who published an earlier version of this book in Italian in 2006;

Thomas Dwyer and his team at the University of Michigan Press for their great support regarding this current version;

Shanly Dixon and Kelly Boudreau who have revised the manuscript with care and, above all, have helped me have clearer thoughts all along;

Clayton George Bailey for his initial and much appreciated literary advice;

Sébastien Babeux for his comments and great help through our constant nocturnal correspondence;

And everyone else that helped me in one way or another: François Lévesque, Lorenzo Bassanelli, Jean Châteauvert, Carl Therrien, Dan Birlew, Peter Nguyen, Mark J. P. Wolf, Pierre Fontaine, Serge Cardinal, Serge Fortin, and Andréane Morin-Simard.

Contents

Introduction 1

1. Survival Terror 10
2. Characters' Nightmarish Delusions in a Resort Town 33
3. Designers' Cinematic Depiction of a Game World 65
4. Gamers' Terrifying Exploration of *Silent Hill* 95

   Conclusion: An Endless Nightmare 126

   The *Silent Hill* Franchise (1999–2009) 136

   Notes 139

   Glossary 149

   Bibliography and Ludography 151

   Index 159

Introduction

The way is the goal.
—*Theravada Buddhist proverb*

The typical starting point for any discussion about *Silent Hill* is a comparison to *Resident Evil*. Given that Capcom's big hit console series (1996) was introduced before Konami's *Silent Hill* (1999), it was and still is the obligatory reference. However, as the *Official U.S. PlayStation Magazine* stated on the cover of its issue of March 1999, *SH1*[1] was "more than just a Resident Evil Clone" (quoted in Davison 2001, 130). At the time, the technical and aesthetic progress was the first thing noticed. The 2-D prerendered realistic backgrounds of Raccoon City were replaced by *Silent Hill*'s real-time 3-D environments. In addition, the fixed camera angles began to move in a dynamic fashion. Although both titles aspired to create a cinematic horror experience, the references were not the same. *Resident Evil* has always been compared to *Night of the Living Dead* (George A. Romero, 1968) and *Silent Hill* to *The Exorcist* (William Friedkin, 1973). This comparison also enabled the differentiation of the overarching scenario of each series: in one, members of Special Tactics and Rescue Service are progressively uncovering the evil doings of "the Umbrella Corporation" and battling a cadre of flesh-eating zombies and biotech monstrosities; in the other, ordinary individuals[2] are caught up in the evil plan of a religious cult known as "The Order" and have to battle monsters and other humanoid creatures that spring forth from the supernatural power of tortured minds. These narrative frameworks eventually gave birth to two different games. *Resident Evil* is more action-oriented, focusing on quick thrill jumps, scares, and gory images, while *Silent Hill* is devised to be more psychological in nature, more about character and atmosphere, intending to convey a tone of dread, anxiety, and helplessness.

Since playing games can become a passion, discussing *Silent Hill* with specific reference to *Resident Evil* (or vice versa) often leads to inflamed debate. Various fan sites and discussion forums are the theater of such clashes. Reviewers also frequently refer to one game or another to express their opinions. For example, Michael Riser's web review of *SH3* (2003):

> Stretching aesthetically beyond the confines of the genre, the first two *Silent Hill* games occasionally felt more about experience and reflection than actual gameplay, but they have enjoyed a large cult following since their inception. Whilst I loathe making this completely inevitable comparison, there are still many who continue to hold *Resident Evil*'s zombie-blasting mediocrity in higher regard simply because the gameplay can feel a touch more focused. These are the same people who don't really understand what the *Silent Hill* games are all about, either because they don't try very hard, don't want to, or simply don't (personal taste plays a part in all things, no less here than anywhere). This isn't to make fans of the series sound like elitists, for all the *Silent Hill* games have had their share of flaws, but this is more to show that it takes a certain kind of person to enjoy a trip to the Hill. No matter how much the games are praised or chastened, there will always be those who hate or love them for various and completely valid reasons. But if you're one who's willing (and brave enough) to spend some time in thought about the series' demented subject matter, you may find yourself wallowing in a deeper experience than you bargained for.

These remarks illustrate an ongoing polemical mode of inquiry that I will forego. I will however, use a portion of Riser's comments as my point of departure. The extraordinary power of *Silent Hill,* as many reviewers have noted, lies in the fact that the series isn't simply a game but rather a uniquely powerful emotional experience.[3] In the *Making of SH2* (Beuglet 2001), the subtitle *Alchemists of Emotion* really is an appropriate title, referring as it does to the now famous "Team Silent," the development team responsible for the first four games of the series.[4] It is for this dimension that millions of copies of the *Silent Hill* series have been sold to date. Therefore, although I'll be discussing *SH: Origins* (2007), *SH: Homecoming* (2008), and *SH: Shattered Memories* (2009), as well as talking about *SH4: The Room* (2004) in the conclusion—and explaining why I do it at this late point, this book will deal primarily with the emotions inherent in *SH1*, *SH2* (2001), and *SH3*, the three games that set the core game mechanics that make the series what it is. I will not focus on the induced stress common to all video games, but instead investigate the specific fears survival horror games are designed to provoke.

An Experiential Route of Fear

My recollection of the beginning of *SH2*[5] is exceedingly clear.[6] I've never been as terrified as the moment I walked down the dark corridor (the brightness level set at 3 as usual) on the second floor of the Wood Side Apartments and began to hear the radio make its static noise. It was "too dark to read the map" (the in-game answer to my command). I had to kill the roaring monster that walked toward James—the player character, after which I ran under a neon light in order to further ponder my exploration. Grazing the walls and pressing my search button, I ended up in a dark room (Room 208) wondering how I was supposed to proceed in this condition. I had a few other interrogations and passed another panicked interlude in front of a second monster before I finally got to Room 205, where I found Mary's dress with the flashlight.[7] This was such a great relief.

We can all agree that there is a big difference between the search I've just described and its alternative, where, for example, we know the flashlight is in Room 205 (and we know that at one point we will find this flashlight from our previous playing of *SH1* and from the manual). This investigative process within the game is not unlike the approaches that one can choose when studying a narrative work: to consider the work as it was experienced in the course of its first reading/viewing (an online perception) or to analyze its overall structure afterward outside of its time flow (a leisurely analysis).[8] Those approaches are informed by cognitive film theory, which I will draw upon in my analysis. Torben Grodal has introduced two metaphors that perfectly elucidate this difference in video gameplay. In order to sum up the two poles in the game experience, poles that demarcate the experience of a newcomer[9] from one who has mastered a game, versus gameplay experienced primarily either as mimesis or as art (or as a program we might add), Grodal differentiates the "game as an experiential route" and the "game as a map and as a system" (2003, 144).

It is certainly beneficial to know our way around, and it would be difficult to write about games while making only vague comments about the action and the places where it transpires. Despite this, it is not my intent to particularize the "map" or virtual environments of Silent Hill and to localize every feature. Nor is my intention to trace the path(s) as in a walkthrough. As we know, each game has different endings[10] that depend on what one does and which items one acquires within the game. For instance, the Konami official website indicated that the first four endings of *SH1* depend on a combination of two conditions, which are whether or not you could see Kaufmann at the motel office, and your ability to save Cybil. Therefore, if you did not get the red liquid on the floor of the Director's office of the Alchemilla Hospital, you will not be able to save Cybil at the merry-go-round. In order to save her, you'll have to replay the game or, obviously, start again midway at the hospital's reception, and so on. Yet, as linear in their structure as the games are, the endings lack finality; they are only provisional.[11] The first three *Silent Hill* games have been described at the time of their release as the "scariest game ever made."[12] This essential affective project—to scare the gamer—is inherent in the experiential route of the gamer in the course of the game(s): it is a lonely psychological journey that drags the gamer into a wealth of nightmarish scenarios.

It is also not my ambition to study the "system" or the programming specifics of the games. In any case, I would be incapable of doing so because, as a gamer, I do not have access to this type of information. My approach remains gamer- or gameplay-centric. The *Silent Hill 3 Official Strategy Guide* (Birlew 2004) does, however, disclose a part of the math behind the game.[13] The user learns the number of points associated with the monsters' overall strength and with the damaging power of Heather's various weapons. For example, the Insane Cancers, huge and fat humanoid creatures, have 2100–2500 physical strength points in normal action level (2520–3000 on hard level). Knowing that the attack power of one handgun bullet is 100 points, one may calculate that it will take more than 20 bullets to kill those monsters. Furthermore, one of their two-hand downward swings has 15 attack power points (a power that will increase throughout the game). Since Heather has 100 physical strength points in normal and hard action level, an Insane Cancer could kill her with 7 swings. Writing for a strategy guide, Birlew suggests the gamer "use this information to make wise decisions regarding when to fight and when to run. Just as each monster has a number representing physical strength, so does Heather. Although this point system is hidden in the game, you can use it to your advantage if you are aware of it" (2004, 8). What's more, the user discovers that *SH3* has a hidden supply balancing system.[14] To maintain the challenge throughout the game, the system counts the ammunition and the number of health items held so as to place or remove certain supplies. Birlew gives the conditional items labels and recommends they be used "to determine why you did or did not find certain conditional supplies while playing through a stage" (2004, 47). For example, the gamer must enter the Hazel Street Station with less than 50 ammunition points, each handgun bullet being worth one point. Once more, Birlew advises the gamer:

> Sometimes it is in your best interests to waste one or two extra rounds or gulp down an extra Health Drink before proceeding to the next stage. For instance, if you leave the Happy Burger with only 54 bullets, it would be wiser to pop off five rounds and enter the Hazel Station with only 49 bullets. The two extra boxes of ammunition that appear on the trashcan near the bathrooms total 20 rounds. Basically, you are trading up. Make the same decision with your recovery items before entering each new stage. Remember that ammunition loaded in the gun counts as well. (2004, 74)

With this kind of knowledge, it is certainly possible to progress through the game more easily. Nevertheless, even though game playing is all about a discrete set of choices, literally calculating all of the moves (as in the upgrade system of a role-playing game) does not elicit the same experience as making a decision based solely on observations or impressions confined to the games. Confronted with a virtual 3-D world as realistic as that of *SH3*, one's initial inclination is to apply real-world thinking. Likewise, encountering terrifying monsters, one's first reaction is not to view them as an algorithm of physical strength points. Those sorts of calculations are secondary (and might be taken into consideration after many attempts to beat a boss).

Who Is Walking (and Running) into *Silent Hill*?

I contend that the design of *Silent Hill*, in contrast to Riser's previous comment about the not rightly focused gameplay, perfectly determines the form of its gameplay. According to the three general attitudes of play that I have defined in a previous essay, the locale of Silent Hill is not for a *gameplayer* (Perron 2003, 251–53), a gamer that would play *with the* game, an agent appropriating the formal structure of the game and essentially playing according to his goals and actions. As opposed to games that take full advantage of procedural authorship[15] such as the famous *Grand Theft Auto* series (Rockstar North / Rockstar Games), *Silent Hill* does not enable the gamer to engage in challenges other than those created by the designers. The gamer might very well decide to shoot at everything, but this will simply exhaust the store of ammunition to no purpose. He cannot, for example, set himself a challenge to shoot out every shop window (they are armor-plated) or cut down all the trees with the chainsaw in a replay game of *SH1* and *SH2* (the blade cleaves through the air). He cannot go beyond the blocked streets. He cannot commit suicide by jumping off the bridge on Bloch Street in *SH1* or aim his rifle at himself whenever a situation becomes unbearable (we are in a *survival* horror game). He cannot intermingle with nonplayer characters (NPCs) since the interactions with them happen in cut-scenes. He can however decide to kill Maria when she follows him in *SH2*, but that ends the game. Yet, if *Silent Hill* does not let the gamer create the path through the game world, it does let him choose how he navigates the given world. The gamer can take the attitude of a *player* (Perron 2003, 244–51), improvising his way as much as possible, wandering freely around town and the various indoor locations. The detailed, real-time 3-D environment has been the chief draw of the series from the beginning. The games allow the player to simply walk around just to experience the graphics, forgetting for a while the goal of the search. This is a point I will return to later given its importance in differentiating survival horror gameplay: the actions of the *player* are observed in survival horror games.

All things considered, *Silent Hill* is designed for the archetypical gamer (Perron 2003, 242–44), that is, a pathfinder striving to traverse a zigzag narrative and who is required to fight monsters and various opponents. As Espen Aarseth has clearly pointed out (2003), one has to decide upon the type of gamer that he will be. Adding the *cheater* to the list, Aarseth is referring to Richard Bartle's (2006) four types of players to describe different styles of play: the *achievers* whose main goal is to accumulate points and/or rise levels; the *explorers* whose chief delight is in forcing the game to reveal its internal machinery; the *socializers* who are interested in making connections to others and social communication; and the *killers* who derive pleasure through dominating gameplay and related interaction. Although this typology was created to study multiuser real-time virtual worlds and therefore has to be adapted to single-player games (gamers and player characters don't socialize much in survival horror games), I must admit that I do not really fit into any of those categories. For instance, I'm not a *cheater*. Even though, to use Aarseth's words, I consult walkthroughs "from time to time," I've never employed GameShark codes or other cheat codes (what's the point of having infinite ammunition in a survival anyway?!).[16] I'm not an *achiever*. I never thought about playing *Silent Hill* in order to have the "10-Star Ranking"[17] and I always chose the normal difficulty level, both for action and riddles. I'm not really an *explorer*. I do sometimes like to play a game again in order to unlock extras or see alternate endings, but this is not my main replay value. I'm not a *killer* either. This might be why I prefer *Silent Hill* to *Resident Evil*, because it's more a question of running away (but not hiding away as in the *Clock Tower* series, for example) from monsters than blowing their heads off. In fact, in keeping with Aarseth's definition of the adventure gamer, I consider myself more of an *intriguee*, the target of the intrigue (1997, 112–14). Though I come from a film studies background, I do have a bias in favor of story-driven games with a connection to cinema. It does not bother me to play the role of innocent, voluntary target[18] of an ergodic intrigue or secret plot in which the possible outcomes depend on my clever actions. As an *intriguee*, I want to go through the multidimensional event space of the game and uncover its structure by negotiating this space. Apposite to this, Aarseth compares this unfolding to "the concept of a log, a recording of a series of experienced events" (1997, 114). In a survival horror game, I want this series of events to be truly frightening. I have replayed *Silent Hill* many times, particularly *SH2*, which I consider a masterpiece, primarily because it sent chills down my spine. Which leads me to the concept of experiential route.

To Get a Fright

In *Emotion and the Structure of Narrative Film: Film as an Emotion Machine*, one of my main theoretical references and the inspiration for the title of the present book (along with the Emotion Engine processor at the heart of the PlayStation 2), Ed S. Tan states that "from the perspective of the viewer, it could be said that what all natural viewers of the traditional feature film have in common is their desire to experience emotion as intensively and as abundantly as possible, within the safe margins of guided fantasy and closed episode" (1996, 39). He defines two types of induced emotion: first, fiction emotions, which are rooted in the fictional world with the concerns addressed by that world, and second, artifact emotions, which arise from concerns related to the artifact, as well as stimulus characteristics based on those concerns (1996, 65). These distinctions structure chapters 2 and 3. Addressed in conversation with Noël Carroll's curiosity theory of fictional works of horror and the pleasures of ratiocination (1990), chapter 2 discusses the setting and story of *Silent Hill*, the way the gamer empathizes with the main protagonists (Travis, Harry, Heather, James, Henry, and Alex), and the impure nature and disgusting aspects of the monsters. Chapter 3 moves toward Grodal's conception of the game as map and system. "Our experience of 'art,'" says Grodal, "is based on our insight into the way in which a given creator realizes specific intentions that are only fully understandable as a choice selected among several possible options, and this demands expertise" (2003, 144). As "audio-video" games, the games of *Silent Hill* often force the gamer to be aware of the game's design (especially gamers with a film perspective like myself), to marvel at their graphics and their mise-en-scène. Chapter 3 investigates the aesthetic aspects of the series.

Although survival horror enthusiasts have a desire to experience fear as intensively and as abundantly as possible, and fiction emotions and artifact emotions are appropriate to video game studies, they can neither be considered straightforwardly nor be thought of as sufficient for the task. As an *intriguee*, I have a certain degree of control over the perception and the unfolding of the action. This notion of agency is central to the differentiation between film and video games in general, and particularly as it relates to the survival horror genre. As Tanya Krzywinska observes, film "is unable to exploit the potential of interactive devices to intensify an awareness of the dynamic between *being in control* and *out of control*, and this aspect is key to the specific types of suspense and emotion-based pleasures offered by horror games" (2002, 215–16). One can only agree with her assertion that "the interactive dimension of these particular games [*Resident Evil 3: Nemesis* (Capcom / Capcom 1999) and *Clive Barker's Undying* (ELEA / EA Games 2001)] is organized to intensify and extend the types of emotional and affective experiences offered by the horror film" (2002, 207). Chapter 4 therefore deals with what I will call gameplay emotions (see for instance Perron 2005a), which arise from the actions of the gamer in the game world and the reaction of this game world to those actions. I will address the role of navigation, battle, use of weapons, solution to riddles, and so on.

But to begin with, I summarize in chapter 1 the distinguishing formal characteristics of the survival horror genre as they appear in *Silent Hill*. To refer to the warning at the beginning of *SH1:* "There are violent and disturbing images in this [book]. The fear of blood tends to create fear for the flesh."

CHAPTER 1

Survival Terror

> Terror is the widening of perspective and perception.
> —David Drayton in Stephen King's The Mist

A Perfect Genre

The survival horror (and let's accept forthright the label even if it has been criticized)[1] is maybe the video game genre *par excellence*. There are many reasons—some more clear-cut than others—to make this claim. First and foremost, as the game designer of *The Suffering* (Surreal Software / Midway 2004) and *The Suffering: Ties That Bind* (Surreal Software / Midway 2005) Richard Rouse III states: "It isn't by accident that so many games have found success in the horror setting. The goals of video games and the goals of horror fiction directly overlap, making them ideal bedfellows" (2009, 15). Moreover, video games rely on the same foundations that many suspense-driven horror films such as *Night of the Living Dead* (George A. Romero, 1968), *Alien* (Ridley Scott, 1979), and *Ringu* (Hideo Nakata, 1998) rely upon.

> Through its actions, this antagonistic force [of horror films] shows itself to be so thoroughly inhuman that no audience member would fault the hero for killing the evil as an act of self defense. This exactly maps on to the experience most action-oriented designers want to create, going all the way back to *Space Invaders;* the player is thrown into a dangerous situation with a clear, undeniable "kill to survive" motivation. The evil forces are numerous and all deserve to die. Hence horror games are a natural fit. (Rouse 2009, 16)

To paraphrase Rouse's essay title, the "match made in hell" is as inevitable as it is successful.

To be true to the genre, survival horror games should be played at night when you are "alone in the dark," and even better, when everyone else is asleep. If this requirement puts the gamer in the same receptive state as the film spectator, it does not lead to an experience similar to cinema, an experience that is always a collective one through the relations of the hero with others (relations expressed among others through shots / reverse shots, i.e., switches between people interacting). Jean-Sébastien Chauvin explains:

> The video game is organized according to an inverse schema: to the collective, it opposes an onanistic experience of the fiction, secret and solitary. It is a time where there is no more than oneself and a (the) world. To this measure, the Survival Horror genre (Silent Hill, Resident Evil) could well be the quintessence of this age of solitude, since when one is there, one is literally, the last of Men. The solitary experience of the character mirrors the player's experience, where both mind and body are engaged by the manipulation of the controller, from which emerge vibrations linked to the context of the game (heart poundings, physical pain). Here, one properly experiences the self. (2002, 39; my translation)[2]

"Quintessence of this age of solitude," survival horror well and truly puts forward the fact that the emotional experience of a video game is a personal one. In the dark, controlling your player character, you are the only one negotiating the menacing game space and facing the monsters.

We can easily imagine that to those who are afraid of video games and only see their evil influence on children, adolescents, and even adults,[3] the survival horror is truly frightening. Indeed, you may remember the 1993–94 Senate hearings regarding the use of violence to promote video games. In a first judgment of 2002, it was upon viewing excerpts from two (out of four) survival horror games—*Fear Effect* (Kronos Digital Entertainment / Eidos Interactive 2000) and *Resident Evil*—that an American federal judge denied video games the protection of free speech, that is, the right guaranteed by the First Amendment of the U.S. Constitution.[4] In addition, in the UK, as reported by Steven Poole, a member of Parliament tried in 1999 to limit the sales of *SH1* because its "story centers on the disappearance and torture of a young girl" (2000, 219). *Silent Hill: Homecoming* has also been banned in Australia in its original gory state (Ramsay 2008). To argue against this hostility, which is itself a by-product of fear, we could take a look at the games from the survival angle.

Play is as much an innate predisposition as an important activity for both our species and other nonhuman mammals, insofar as this activity only occurs because the participants are capable of some degree of metacommunication (exchanging signals that say, for instance, "This is play" and not a real fight). Bateson has observed that "the evolution of play may have been an important step in the evolution of communication" (1972, 181). As he pointed out, learning to recognize a threat leads to being able to foresee and prevent the denoted potential attack. Torben Grodal has summarized this evolutionary perspective by showing how "our ability to empathize with, identify with, and cognitively [and above all virtually in video games] simulate the situation of other members of our species is linked to *the evident survival value of these prosocial activities*" (Grodal 1997, 86; emphasis added). Without the fatal consequences of "ordinary" or real life, it is possible in the virtual space of video games to try out and observe the effects of different behaviors (for instance, being aggressive when it is not in your nature), test different strategies for problem solving (in a problematic and unsafe situation: charge in, run in zigzags to avoid being attacked, slowly bypass unnecessary confrontations, etc.), live in danger, and experience strong feelings. Opportunities to encounter disgusting and abnormal creatures like those of *Silent Hill* are limited in our daily life, but the techniques for dealing with a survival situation probably remain similar. As studies have shown, video games enhance visual processing[5] and can even be effective for overcoming phobias.[6]

It's difficult to overcome fears. In the famous words of master of horror H. P. Lovecraft, which I have quoted elsewhere (Perron 2005b),[7] fear is "the oldest and strongest emotion of mankind . . . and the oldest and strongest kind of fear is fear of the unknown" (1973, 12). What's more, "As may naturally be expected of a form so closely connected with primal emotion, the horror-tale is as old as human thought and speech themselves" (1973, 17). To the adversaries of supernatural horror tales, Lovecraft retorted with a response that is worth quoting again both to give a certain status to the genre and to respond to academic colleagues outside of video game studies who do not understand why you're wasting your time playing video games, doubly so by playing horror games:

> The appeal of the spectrally macabre is generally narrow because it demands from the reader [or the gamer] a certain degree of imagina-

tion and a capacity for detachment from everyday life. Relatively few are free enough from the spell of the daily routine to respond to rappings from outside, and tales of ordinary feelings and events, or common sentimental distortions of such feeling and event, will always take first place in the taste of the majority. (1973, 12)

It is not just anyone who can enjoy horror fiction. The objects of fascination of the genre are impure, disgusting, and scary monsters. The natural inclination is to move away, not to advance toward those beings who call for both a cognitive engagement, so as to try to discover this very fearful unknown, and an imaginative engagement, in which one is willing to "creatively speculat[e] about what the monster might be like, what it might want and how it might be managed" (Vorobej 1997, 238).[8] More specific to the video game, it forces a virtual physical engagement since the gamer, through his/her player character, will have to manage the monsters on his/her own. Those engagements make explicit the noteworthy observation of Janet Murray concerning fiction. For Murray, the expression commonly used to describe the pleasure of immersion in a imaginative world, Coleridge's "willing suspension of disbelief," constitutes too passive a formulation. The question is more about an "active creation of belief" since we use our intelligence to strengthen the reality of the experience (Murray 1997, 110). Without a doubt, the pleasure of playing, to reiterate, also depends on "being played." You play a survival horror game because you want to be scared. As Jonathan Lake Crane underlines regarding horror films, if you don't "manufacture particular kinds of belief" (1994, 47) and if you remain distant or turn your back on the imaginary dangerous world, the game is over even before it has started.

Drawing upon the concept made famous by Jay David Bolter and Richard Grusin (2002), the video game has *remediated* the film. This videoludic refashioning of cinematic forms could not have been more evident with regard to horror. It's true that all genres are characterized by a set of pre-established conventions generating a certain number of more or less precise expectations. In this perspective, the notion of genre stimulates a certain reflexive game of guesswork and recognition. However, of all the genres, it may be argued that horror is the one most often compared to a game. In light of Bateson's theory of play and fantasy, the depiction of horror has to be framed as a playful and fictional activity since it would be neither tolerated nor bearable otherwise (which is the case of *snuff* movies, where showing the actual murder of a human being renders them intolerable and unacceptable to the general viewer—the antithesis to playful). To find pleasure in horror film, it is necessary to play by its rules. This is why, while many scholars have sporadically made references to a game analogy in order to explain the contemporary horror film experience, others like Ruth Amossy and Vera Dika have made a lengthy and narrower link that is also worth presenting.

Ruth Amossy associates the horror tales to play and games in a chapter of *Les idées reçues: Sémiologie du stéréotype* (1991) dealing with the industrialization of fear. She states that the "art of frightening" is openly put forward as a ludic activity. She then lists three categories of objects of fear: (1) transgressions of normality and elementary laws of the physical known world like the "Old Ones" of Lovecraft or King Kong; (2) harmless objects in themselves that become scary only through an abnormal and strange aggressive behavior, such as birds, furniture, and cars; and (3) objects already scary that undergo a hyperbolic processing, such as wolves, spiders, and snakes. This closed repertoire of fear and the fundamental use of stereotypes therefore serve as "direction signs of the ludic domain. They announce at the entry and at critical points of the fictional terror: 'All those that enter here accept surrender to the dizziness of fear'" (1991, 142; my translation). To clarify the activity at stake, Amossy refers to board games:

> The progress of the game is not purely fortuitous, and the public expects that some "moves" mark out the itinerary of fear. . . . [The] threatening interruptions [by objects of fear] in the daily universe and adventures that ensue are also meticulously programmed according to known rules. One thinks of those games where the participants have, with throws of dice, to cross a perilous space sown with ambushes until they reach the square of final resolution.
>
> If, therefore, the imitated reality is not defined by precise rules, the precise delineation of the terror will bring some to bear. It is the grid of the laws of terror applied on daily and banal scenery, or at least on what is claimed to be realistic, that produces the narrative of terror. (1991, 138; my translation)

On any given game board, the moves differ, but the grid remains the same.[9] What happens next always maintains some kind of predictability. According to Amossy, the secret of the industry of fear lies less in the choice of the stereotyped object than in the choice of representation. Cinema thus occupies a preponderant place since it constantly invents and perfects its realistic effects. The conclusions of Amossy put Steven Poole's reasoning in perspective:

> Why is it particularly the horror genre, and to a lesser extent science-fiction, that largely provides the aesthetic compost for supposedly "film-like" videogames? ... The answer is that horror genre can easily do away with character and plot; it is the detail of the monster, the rhythm and tension and shocks that matter. Plot and characters are things video-games find very difficult to deal with. (2000, 79)

For the video game, a new media that is still audiovisual, the horror film provides a breeding ground for formal figures and techniques of mise-en-scène (anxiety-provoking music, expressive high/low angles, suspicious camera movements, startle effects, etc.). It also provides an ideal narrative framework: a small group of stereotypical characters barricade themselves in a place—or try to escape—in order to fight against and to survive an evil force embodied in monsters or ghosts. This perfectly suits the video game (the new media), which will inevitably, as did cinema (the old media), continuously invent and refine its realistic effects (in connection with computer manufacturers who constantly endeavor to sell new state-of-the-art technology).

Vera Dika has dedicated her book *Games of Terror: Halloween, Friday the 13th, and the Films of the Stalker Cycle* to demonstrating the way in which the stalker film formula of the 1980s put the spectator in a condition "less like watching a tennis match, for example, than like playing a *video game.* Here the spectator is implicated by a number of conventional formal strategies, ones that encourage a play with the film itself" (1990, 22; emphasis added). For Dika, the formal opacity of the repeated patterns and the surface variations (point-of-view shots, use of onscreen and offscreen spaces, frameline, screen time, etc.) facilitate a gaming attitude toward two central questions: "Where is the killer?" and "When will he strike?" Starting with *Halloween* (John Carpenter, 1978) and its two best copies *Friday the 13th* (Sean S. Cunningham, 1980) and *Friday the 13th Part 2* (Steve Miner, 1981), the safe and controlled interaction between the spectator and the stalker-film games established a play of knowing or not knowing the answer to those two questions, and of how they were asked. Such play has become even more pervasive in the new cycle of stalker films initiated by the self-reflexive *Scream* (Wes Craven, 1996), a cycle created for a generation of teenagers who are as much film and television viewers as they are gamers.

As Amossy's reference to game boards and Dika's video game analogy show, the contemporary horror film was already playful and "interactive" before the advent of video games and explicit interactivity. It was a short leap to make "interactive horror movies" such as *Phantasmagoria* (Sierra / Sierra, 1995) or *Realms of the Haunting* (Gremlin Interactive / Interplay, 1996). Moreover, when asked how he would like *SH2* to be seen, the producer Akihiro Imamura answered: "As a horror movie, but with the fantastic feeling of being active within it" (Roundell 2001). With an action-oriented narrative framework and all the prominently displayed formal "direction signs" along the experiential route to fear, the spectator-gamer was more than ready to get into the labyrinth of horror and virtually display his competitive spirit.

The relation between survival horror games and horror films underlines a central element of play and games, which is repetitiveness. As we've seen, there is a horror formula, and anyone who is even marginally familiar with the genre is aware of this fact. However, Noël Carroll made a point of noting, in his transmedia study, that "predictability does not deter the horror audience's interest (indeed, audiences would appear to desire that the same stories be told again and again)" (1990, 97–98). It's precisely the noticeable variations within the framework, the efficacious scare tactics and the novelty of the techniques, that thrill horror enthusiasts and reaffirm their appreciation for the genre; it is a way simultaneously both to maintain and to lose control over the experience. This remark can be applied to many video games. To begin with Warren Robinett's groundbreaking video (or graphic) game *Adventure* for the Atari 2600 (Atari, 1979)—not forgetting the text and text-and-graphic adventures that have preceeded and followed Robinett's game—adventures are designed on the same model: in a large mazelike game world, a player character/protagonist has to solve various problems and use various tools to get past obstacles and fight enemies in order to succeed in his quest to find something or to save someone. In this type of game environment, it's stunningly realistic graphics and the expandable exploring environment that succeed for the gamer. With their own variations and chief characteristics, many action games (first- or third-person shooters) and role-playing games still follow this adventure formula. As for survival horror—sometimes called horror adventure—it shades the adventure with nerve-racking, morbid, and dark features. There is a last reason to see survival horror as an exemplary genre.

> The adventure maze embodies a classic fairy-tale narrative of danger and salvation. Its lasting appeal as both a story and a game pattern derives from the melding of cognitive problem (finding the path) with emotionally symbolic pattern (facing what is frightening and unknown).... Like all fairy tales, the maze adventure is a *story about survival*. The maze is the road map for telling this story. (Murray 1997, 130; emphasis added)

Survival horror clearly exhibits the ins and outs of a broad range of video games.

Slowly Getting into a World of Survival Horror

Even if we establish 1992 as the date of the origin of the survival horror genre, we still have to go back to the horror games of the 1980s to construct an accurate genealogy of the genre.

Drawing from Robinett's design, James Andreasen's *Haunted House* (Atari, 1981) gave the adventure genre its first pitch-black representation. If it is difficult to see anything when progressing through the catacombs of *Adventure* (depicted as an orange-pathed network); it is also hard to explore each of the six rectangular rooms in the four-story-high *Haunted House*'s mysterious mansion. As a pair of square eyes (compared to the little square of *Adventure*), you have to discover the three pieces of a magic urn and bring it back to the house's entrance. In your search, with nine lives and an unlimited supply of matches to see your way around (giving a reddish diamond-form view), you also need to find a master key to open locked doors, protect yourself with a magic scepter, or fight tarantulas, vampire bats, and ghosts. As the manual warns the gamer: "Every time one of these creatures touches you, you'll be 'scared to death,' and consequently lose a life."[10] To suggest this effect and to create a horror "atmosphere," *Haunted House* uses flickering lights and thunderclaps when you are touched (your eyes will roll wildly). It also capitalizes on other specific sound effects, such as the sound of wind when creatures approach (which also blows out your matches), creaking doors, a knock every time you slam into walls and locked doors, and—says the manual again—"a spooky tune" (three notes in fact) when you use the stairs. Nine game variations challenge your scoring based on the number of matches you use and the number of lives you have left at the end of the game.

While the scrolling of *Haunted House* is mainly vertical in a very limited space (three rectangular double-rooms), other games had a horizontal layout so as to give a more "realistic" sense of the scene. Since stalker films were mentioned earlier, let's refer to the Atari 2600 video game adaptation of *Halloween* (Wizard Video Games, 1983). In the game, the player character has three lives to navigate adjacent spaces representing the sixteen rooms of a two-story house (upper and lower levels accessible through connecting doors). She is a babysitter trying to save as many children as possible from the killer, who may appear anywhere, and bring them to safe rooms. Each child saved gives the gamer 675 points toward his total score. Occasionally, she finds a knife that enables her to defend herself. It is not mentioned (either on the box or in the manual) that the killer is Michael Myers, but his pale blue suit indicates that connection (sadly, it's not possible to recognize Jamie Lee Curtis). In fact, the player character and the NPCs start to look like human figures. The "terrified children" (manual) wave their two-pixels arms and Michael brandishes his three-pixel knife and everybody moves their little feet. This initial level of anthropomorphism is giving birth to the first images of "gore" because at the moment Michael stabs the babysitter, he cuts her head off and leaves her running around with a few pixels of blood spurting out of her neck (same thing for children). To enhance the atmosphere of the game, *Halloween* uses the first notes of the movie musical theme every time Michael appears. The effect of his sudden apparitions is increased by an "electrical blackout" (manual), that is, a flickering effect that plunges you into darkness for a few seconds while the killer is pursuing you.

Many other horror video games of the 1980s could be introduced here to support the argument. One could obviously think about horror text adventures like Dave Lebling's *The Lurking Horror* (Infocom / Infocom, 1987) or multiple windows text-and-graphic adventures such as *Shadowgate* (ICOM Simulation / Mindscape, 1987) and *Uninvited* (ICOM Simulation / Mindscape, 1987). Konami's *Castlevania* (1987) is also part of the horror game genre evolution. To maintain a film perspective, the NES adaptation of *Friday the 13th* (LJN, 1989) could have been introduced similarly to Commodore 64's *Project Firestart* (Dynamix / Electronic Arts, 1989), which is also referred to as an ancestor of survival horror.[11] However, one game cannot be overlooked here: the Japanese RPG game *Sweet Home* (Capcom / Capcom, 1989)—released at the same time as its film counterpart realized by Kiyoshi Kurosawa.

One of the primary inspirations for *Resident Evil*, *Sweet Home* follows classical horror patterns. An investigation team travels to the painter Ichirō Mamiya's haunted manor, situated beside a lake, in order to photograph his frescoes. But Mamiya's evil spirit traps them inside the dangerous, corpse-filled, mazelike manor, which the team must search while struggling to survive and escape. Since it is an RPG game, each of three women and two men who you can control (interestingly enough in parties of two or three) has her/his own characteristics (levels of experience, attack power, health points, and pray points, which is another attack device) and her/his own tool that will be necessary to complete the adventure (Taro has a camera, Akiko a first-aid kit, Emi a key, Kazuo a lighter, and Asuka a vacuum cleaner). You can switch between the characters. The main screen of *Sweet Home* shows an overhead view of the manor. To the beat of a few efficacious synthesized musical themes, you scroll through the space with the team in order to find clues, various items, and weapons that are scattered around. A menu of popup commands enables you to look at things, talk to people, manage items, and save your state of play as many times as you wish. Clues are found in objects such as dolls and skeletons, in conversations with zombies or people and mainly in notes, blood messages, and frescoes that have to be cleaned beforehand (by Asuka, or someone else who has a broom) and photographs (by Taro or another camera owner). Various items are needed to overcome obstacles or monsters, such as tonic flasks that restore your life and pray points, pieces of wood or ropes to cross gaps, mallets to destroy rocks, statues, or mirrors, keys to open specific doors, two rings to bypass a guardian, and so on. Four items used in a certain order are necessary to beat the (final) boss, Mamiya. Weapons have different attack powers. However, a player character may possess only one weapon at a time. For that matter, with their initial tools, player characters can carry only four items at a time, and the inventory only has two open slots. Therefore you need to manage your items strategically, giving them to teammates, exchanging them, or drinking your tonic flask in order to leave room for a necessary tool. Following the examples of *Adventure* and *Haunted House*, certain sections of the manor are plunged into darkness, and a wax candle is required to light up a square around your party. Furthermore, similar to *Adventure*'s bat, which could remove objects or people, blue flying balls or ghosts can snatch one player character away and transport him to another room in the manor. Except for blue cats and mice, which don't hurt you, enemies such as flying bats, suits of armor, and mirrors wander around launching attacks if you do not avoid them. However, there are many monsters (corpses, evil dolls, hounds, ghosts, ghouls, worms, zombies, etc.), which are invisible and can at any time take you by surprise. The music changes, the screen turns black, and then the image of the monster appears in an attack screen. You can attack, pray, run (but you will fall down), use a tool, or call upon your teammate during a fight. While the action is under way and damages are displayed, red sparkles on the screen. For example, if one player character is poisoned, red flickering will occur when he moves and Akiko's first-aid kit will be required. Since you do not know which monster is going to show up or (depending on your experience level) how the battle will turn out, particularly with the tougher types, there is always a certain gameplay tension. Classical lighting effects enhance the atmosphere. *Sweet Home* even tries to create an interesting scare effect by making the "Man" enemy suddenly reveal a half-human half-skull face in a two-image switch (from the back of the enemy to the front of his face). It also keeps you on your toes by making things, such as a chair or a light, fall in a shaky image. When you decide to go left or right, to dive or pray, there is always a short lapse of time before you know if you made the right decision.

Although web reviewers have stated that "*Haunted House* still manages to instill a sense of fear and panic in the player" and that *Halloween* "captures the spirit of the movie quite well," and although the first line of the manual of *The Texas Chainsaw Massacre* (Wizard Video Games, 1983) asserts that the game "recreate[s] the chilling climax of the most horrifying movie ever made!" these claims overlook the very limited scary effects of the abstract graphics of those games.[12] Even if we keep a historical distance and regard them for what they are, the same conclusions have to be made about the NES 8-bit graphics[13] or the excellent imagery of *Sweet Home*. All things considered, we have to agree with the assertion made by Win Sical and Remi Delekta[14] in "Survival Horror: Un Nouveau Genre," an article from the first and only issue of the French *Horror Games Magazine*: "Survival horror [can] not exist without a minimum of technical capacities: sounds, graphics, processing speed. Fear, to exist, needs to be staged, and this mise-en-scène requires capabilities" (Sical and Delekta 2003, 13; my translation). This mise-en-scène of fear was fulfilled in 1992 in a French PC game considered to be the first of its breed: *Alone in the Dark* (I-Motion Inc. & Infogrames / Interplay).[15]

This "Virtual Adventure Game Inspired by the Works of H. P. Lovecraft" (box set) and also inspired by the zombie movies of George A. Romero (see

Provezza 2006, 54) takes place in the 1920s and follows the trail of private detective Edward Carnby (or of Hartwood's niece, Emily Hartwood, but it is not possible to switch from one to the other as in *Sweet Home*) in a haunted mansion called Derceto where the former owner, Jeremy Hartwood, who was translating ancient occult manuscripts, hanged himself. Since devil worship makes Carnby smile, he looks for Derceto's terrible secret, which results in his having to fight evil creatures. It is certainly not on those narrative premises that *Alone in the Dark* should be considered innovative. It is the means of the game that changed things. Indeed, *Alone in the Dark* is the first game to display 3-D polygonal characters and objects in 2-D pre-rendered 256-color backgrounds. This feature results in the game depicting a better immersive horror world and, above all, a remediated cinematic one since the action is always depicted from different fixed camera angles (as the expressionistic vertical angle—compared to a flat overhead view as in *Sweet Home*—which shows the character trapped in a corridor maze). For instance, it's a high-angle view that shows Edward's car arriving at Derceto's gate. Then, while Edward is walking toward it, another high-angle long shot of the mansion reveals a light in one of the second-floor windows, followed by its countershot from that window revealing only the hands of what we might guess is a strange creature looking down toward the player character. What's more, this opening cut-scene is an exceptional preview of the way in which gameplay is enacted. All of the shots, mainly typical views from the ceiling, which are used to lead Edward from the main entrance to the attic, disclose spaces that you will pass through later on, not without sudden, unexpected events. Thus, although the graphics of the game look primitive in comparison to today's standards and the music and sound effects do not have the same range, *Alone in the Dark* is still viewed as one of the "scariest games ever" because, as noted, it stages fear. The musical orchestration is compelling right from the beginning and varies during the game. You hear howls or strident sounds once in a while. The squeaking doors close heavily behind Edward. Floors creak. Footsteps produce quiet echoes in the tunnel. When you begin to explore the attic, you hear a sudden musical chord and see (or the game will cut to it) a long-fanged monster breaking through the window to attack you. Later on, a shot from outside a bedroom window brings yet another monster through it, a monster that will even jump on the bed to attack you.

In *Alone in the Dark,* the way a room is framed is sometimes employed as a technique to hide monsters from sight, as is the case when the long-fanged monster appears[16] and attacks you, just after you've taken Jeremy Hartwood's notebook in his first room. In the kitchen cupboard, while a low-angle shot from the coal on the floor shows Edward, a zombie suddenly appears behind him. This kind of cinematographic mise-en-scène is based on a third-person perspective. In that sense, one has to agree with Daniel S. Yu that this perspective is more appropriate to survival horror games. As he says regarding *Alone in the Dark* in "Exploring the Survival Horror Genre":[17]

> Beyond the usual annoying aspects (like views changing during fights), the third person perspective added to the dramatic tension by allowing the player to see things that would otherwise be lost in a first person perspective, such as monsters chasing the player character and the player character running for his/her life at the same time. (Yu 2002)

In the third-person perspective, you have to think in relation to the player character, considering the actions he is capable of performing (Edward can run, fight barehanded, raise a rifle to his shoulder and shoot, open/search, shut doors, push large objects, jump, use items and throw/drop/place them) and of his relation to the camera: Is he close or far from the camera? Do his movements involve a change of angle? Does that limit the gamer's vision? Is the player character in an open space where he can run or in a room where he can be caught? And so on. There is also the dimension of the body, its movements, its strength or vulnerability, and the violence to which the body is subjected. It is easy to be overcome by panic in first- and third-person perspectives while being attacked by a monster, but you're more effectively overcome by horror when you actually see your player character out of your control being (b)eaten to death in a corner and dragged along the ground by a zombie to the stone altar (an end sequence that might have inspired one in *SH3*). This way of visualizing is more "film-like" and is naturally associated with the horror genre.

The gameplay of *Alone in the Dark* shows all the elements that will define the survival horror genre. To begin with, there is no map of the mansion available so you have to memorize the location of various rooms. You can switch to two screens. The first is the "save, load, quit and parameter screen" (manual). It is, notably, possible to save and reload anytime during the game (before a fight, an investigation, or after every jump onto pillars). The second is the "options screen," which has three frames: one for the inventory, one for the possible actions, and one that shows your player character's life points and the selected items. The inventory is limited; therefore it's important to manage the items that you'll choose to take with you. To save space it's possible to combine them. For example, you'll need to use the oilcan to fill the lamp and the matches to light it. This lamp is essential to investigate a dark bedroom in order to find (1) a heavy statuette, (2) the library to get to a secret room, and (3) a maze you have to pass through. Incidentally, like *Adventure* and *Haunted House,* the screen of this maze is entirely black except for a small lit circle around the player character.

As in a standard adventure game, you have to toil through scattered clues that are discovered in books and parchments. The clues explain what happened in Derceto and how to solve the various puzzles encountered. For instance, references to Lovecraft's Cthulhu, his call, and the danger of the infamous Necronomicon are found in books. In order to discover the way to pass by the "medusas" at the top of the stairs you must refer to the first book found and then apply the section that states "shields that may shine like mirrors." J. Hartwood also writes in his notebook about the caverns you need to discover under the house. You have to open various boxes or search the furniture to find items and then collect the objects required to fulfill a particular task, for instance: acquire a gramophone, search for a key to obtain a record album, and finally fight a pirate for the key to get to the ballroom in order to play a dance song. Daniel S. Yu and other reviewers have noticed that there are not very many enemies (Lovecraft's monsters and creatures) to fight in Derceto, but neither are there many health drinks (two and one box of cookies) or ammunition in the game (eight shells and 18 bullets). It is very evident that *Alone in the Dark* is more about survival than horror. In fact, there are fewer pixels of splashing blood, and monsters aren't drenched in blood when they are defeated; they supernaturally vanish in smoke instead. You have to accomplish the final part of the game in the caverns without any new supplies. Additionally, falling into the water cuts down on the items that might be used because the matches and shells get wet. You have to be very careful while making your way back up to the mansion, saving as often as possible and repeating actions that have not been performed perfectly.

The PlayStation game *Resident Evil* (Capcom / Capcom, 1996) popularized the survival horror genre despite the fact that it was preceded by *Alone in the Dark.* If the link between *Resident Evil* and *Alone in the Dark* is not well established, it is the contrary in regards to *Sweet Home.* With its door-opening loading screens, its in-game note saying, "You must escape this house of residing evil!" (seen as an explicit reference), and the fact that the game was played during the development stage, the game released by Capcom in 1989 remains the acknowledged source for *Resident Evil*. Therefore, we can compare the gameplay experiences of these three games and notice significant connections.

Resident Evil opens with the Special Tactics and Rescue Service (S.T.A.R.S.) Alpha team trapped in Spencer Mansion. In order to escape, the team has to confront many zombies and biotech monstrosities (and traitors inside the team). Guided by a map this time, the team's investigations uncover the secret machinations of the Umbrella Corporation. The tasks necessary to achieve their goal include finding clues in notes and documents, pushing things around (as in *Alone in the Dark*), looking for keys and various crests, and acquiring items for specific undertakings. Two player characters are on hand: Chris Redfield and Jill Valentine. As opposed to Edward Carnby or Emily Hartwood, the adventure is not similar for each character. Right from the start of the game, Chris ventures out alone, with only a survival knife to defend himself, while Jill has a gun and is followed by teammate Barry Burton. Without being a RPG, the story revolves around the S.T.A.R.S. team. Jill is helped by Barry at key moments throughout the game, and Chris is aided by Rebecca Chambers (from the Bravo Team). You also come across teammates, one of whom is poisoned by a huge snake and, similar to *Sweet Home,* you'll have to get a serum to try to cure him. If you are the one bitten, you'll have to get the serum in order to survive. Otherwise, you heal yourself with a variety of herbs (green, red, and blue) during the course of the game. You discover from a botany book that these herbs can be mixed to increase their healing power. In the course of action, mixing plants and combining items (weapon and clip, as in *Alone in the Dark*) also saves space in the inventory. The inventory of *Resident Evil*, like its two predecessors, is limited. Chris can carry six items and Jill eight. Therefore, inventory needs to be managed. As opposed to *Alone in the Dark,* it is not possible to drop or throw items anywhere or anytime. Instead, the herbs, weapons (you come across new and more powerful ones), and items have to be stored in boxes near save points. This way, you can retrieve things later in the game. This device complicates your mission and has been criticized on numerous occasions. If Steven Poole finds this inconsistent and laughable (2000, 66), Daniel S. Yu provides a more qualified opinion:

> In truth, this was both good and bad. Good in that it created additional tension by (somewhat arbitrarily) limiting the player's inventory. Bad in

that it tended to "break the illusion" of an interactive horror movie by inadvertently reminding players that they were still playing a game—I have to stash the ammo I can't (for some reason) carry in this arbitrarily placed storage box so I can come back for it later? Say what? (Yu 2002)

Another device became a standard of the survival horror form. Unlike *Sweet Home* and *Alone in the Dark*, it is not possible to save your PlayStation game anytime you choose. In order to save, you are required to find ink ribbons and use them in typewriters that are encountered during your progress. As everyone agrees, having to go from one save point to another, or having to return to a previous one for safety, creates a real and relevant dramatic tension since the whole point of the game is about being afraid to die.

If there is a link to be made between *Alone in the Dark* and *Resident Evil*, it is on the basis of its depiction. *Resident Evil* really did "welcome [you] to the world of survival horror" (read in the intro screen). Its live-action video opening scene demonstrates its propensity to be viewed as an interactive movie. A few shots of a dog's jaws and teeth along with a camera quickly moving toward the panic-stricken teammates set the menacing tone for what comes next. B-movie credits introduce each teammate through real actors who put a face on the polygonal characters. When Chris or Jill meets the first zombie, the prerendered cut-scene (not in the usual letterbox format so as to make it look as in-game) revealing the ugly face of this zombie also states that the game calls out the dark side of horror. *Resident Evil* maximizes the PlayStation graphics capacity and improves on the tricks and aesthetic of the 3-D characters in the 2-D prerendered backgrounds of *Alone in the Dark*. The eerie music and the sound effects (like the different footsteps, gunshots, groans, roars, etc.) have everything it takes to set the mood. Its prerendered backgrounds are very detailed and use light sources and shadows in an expressionist manner (the characters cast only a dark circle on the ground). The cinematic camera angles—many of which are vertical angles—and the various cuts during gameplay also exploit well the architecture of the mansion and trick the gamer. In a scene reminiscent of *Alone in the Dark* and now considered a classic, Jill makes her way down a corridor, music playing in the background. When the camera cuts to the door which Jill has just entered in order to reveal her in a long shot, a dog bursts through the right window in the immediate foreground, making you jump out of your seat. After Jill has killed the beast to the rhythm of fast-paced music and turned the corner, another dog again bursts through a window (a Flying Reptile bursts in a similar way through Cafe 5to2's windows at the beginning of *SH1*). The gamer has to be continuously ready for action in *Resident Evil* because enemies are waiting behind doors or beyond the limits of the frame to surprise and attack her. To perfect its effects, the game draws from the closed repertory of fear, employing Zombies, Zombie Dogs, monsters (such as Chimeras, Hunters, and the T002-Tyrant), and beings that have undergone a hyperbolic processing by the T-Virus (such as the Plant 42, the large Bees, Sharks, Snake, and Spider). The encounters with this bestiary give rise to gory confrontations/episodes. The few pixels representing blood in *Alone in the Dark* are replaced with big spurts. Taking full advantage of the horror intrinsic with the third-person perspective, when Chris or Jill suffers an attack, blood spatters in streams. Despite the fact that the aiming controls are limited in *Resident Evil,* one of the main thrills of the game is to kill the biotech monstrosities, making their heads blow up (as opposed to seeing them blow up as in Romero's movies). As Matthew Weise states in his "The Rules of Horror: Procedural Adaptation in *Clock Tower, Resident Evil,* and *Dead Rising*," which deals with the modeling of horror texts into video games: "Although *Resident Evil* was an extremely limited exploration of the zombie simulation, it did manage to simulate certain aspects of the zombie film for the first time" (2009, 255).

Lurking Fear

There were several survival horror games released in North America between 1996 and 1999, such as *Clock Tower* (Human Entertainment / ASCII Entertainment Software, 1996—the Japanese *Clock Tower 2*), *Overblood* (River Hill Software / Electronic Arts, 1997), *Parasite Eve* (Square Soft / Square Soft, 1998), and, obviously, *Resident Evil 2* (Capcom / Capcom, 1998). These games incorporated new characteristics such as hidden spots, different camera perspectives, outside urban scenes, RPG elements, and injuries that affect the movement of your player character; however, they did not have the same major impact on the genre as *SH1* and its features.

With the exception of an unlimited inventory and a map that is automatically marked as the areas are searched, *SH1* follows the usual cinematic adventure framework as described throughout this chapter using the examples of *Alone in the Dark* and *Resident Evil*. However, because *SH1* takes place inside, outside, and in overlapping real and alternate worlds, it

Fig. 1. *Silent Hill 1:* Harry Mason walking in the dark, over the bottomless abyss of the Otherworld

builds a whole new frightening atmosphere. To render its fully real-time 3-D environments, Team Silent dealt with the finite processing resources of the PlayStation by limiting the field of vision. The fog and darkness are used to hide what is not depicted. As many reviewers have noted, this technical limitation has resulted in one of the most praised aesthetic effects of the game. The feeling of entrapment is very pronounced. You don't see very far when wandering the streets of the resort town. The limits remain uncertain. You are always expecting to run into something awful. When you end up in the Otherworld and the streets change to grates, you are really made to feel as if you were walking over a bottomless abyss (fig. 1).

The dark ambience of Silent Hill is intensified. The flashlight Harry Mason finds at the beginning of the game, at the Cafe 5to2, gives a new signification to a visual trick that can be, as I wished to draw attention to with my quick look at the history of the genre, traced back to *Adventure*. Given that you can only see what you light, you have to be very careful because monsters can be waiting, not only beyond the limits of the frame, but also just outside the real-time light halo. The light can be turned off so as not to alert enemies, plunging you into obscurity and intense fear. *SH1* uses yet another device, audio this time, to heighten the fear. The pocket radio Harry receives before leaving Cafe 5to2 only transmits white noise when there are dangerous creatures nearby. While this prevents many surprise scares (which are still not completely eliminated), it elevates the level of tension. Fear rises every time the static grows louder. Not knowing which direction the monster is coming from, you remain continuously on your guard until you encounter the source of the emission.

Despite all of its peculiarities, *SH1,* and to an even greater extent *SH2,* remains the perfect game of a perfect genre. You truly are "alone in the dark" (and there is no switch to turn on the lights as in *Alone in the Dark: The New Nightmare* [Darkworks / Infogrames 2001]). Fear of the dark comes first in Stephen King's list of ten key fears that underpin the creation of emotion in horror texts (in Wells 2002, 11). *Silent Hill* makes the most of it. You are dealing with yourself in an eerie space while desperately trying to survive through the night. Following the thread of exploration characteristic of the maze adventure, the quest for salvation in the labyrinth implies two movements, one that drives toward the center as in *SH: Origins, SH1, SH: Shattered Memories*, and *SH2,* and another that leads toward the exit as in *SH3*. The gripping city of Silent Hill prompts you to actively create or manufacture fear. The games of the *Silent Hill* series remain in the "Scariest Games Experience Ever"; and there remains even more to discover.

Assessed in comparison to *Resident Evil,* the horror of *SH1* (and of the other games in the series) is best described as being psychological. The entire game is governed more by its atmosphere than by its action, by what is felt rather than by what is done. This design ensues from clear intentions. As Akihiro Imamura, the lead game system programmer of *SH1* (also involved in concept planning, according to Beuglet 2001) and producer of *Silent Hill 2,* says in interviews:

> I am aiming to create fear which gets deep into human instinct. Not making the fear by surprise, but by creating a feeling of anxiety, I would like to surge the fear little by little in the player. (Perry 2001a)

> In *Silent Hill 2,* fear could be defined in terms of what you don't see makes you feel afraid. If you know that there is something around that you can't see, you'll be scared, deep down. (Beuglet 2001)

Masashi Tsuboyama, who worked on *SH1* and directed *SH2,* puts a term on the general atmosphere of the games:

> The existence of fog and darkness and the real and alternate world is an important element in creating fear . . . just as in the previous title. However, for this title, I was conscious of a certain "strangeness" that was present in the game and in our daily lives. What I mean by "strangeness" is unexplained occurrences that can happen on and off without any real reason. Examples within the game would be the existence of [the] red square, the circumstances in which you get the handgun, traffic lights which are turned on in the deserted town, wandering monsters in the real world, buildings of unrealistic structure [though they seem realistic on the surface], etc. Moreover, we incorporated these ideas of "strangeness" throughout the game. . . . It adds a different quality to the oppressive fear already prevalent. (Beuglet 2001)

Team Silent has understood that, as Paul Wells formulates it, "the most persuasive horror is the one suggested in the mind of the viewer [and the gamer], rather than that which is explicitly expressed on the screen" (2002, 108–9). For instance, with the town of *SH1* shrouded in mist and darkness I mistook a fire hydrant for a dangerous dog; I've also been frightened by white noise that finally ended without any sign of danger. I shuddered when I heard the child crying in the boys' restroom of Midwich Elementary School. Without a map, I was thrown into panic when the first door locked itself behind me on the new fourth floor of the Alchemilla Hospital.[18] I could continue with examples, but we're going to come back to that later. Because, on the one hand, if the fairly obvious but hard to achieve requirement of survival horror games is to "be able to deliver dramatic scares to the player continuously throughout the game" (Yu 2002), *Silent Hill* delivers the goods. Indeed, it is not just at the sudden appearance of zombies that the gamer is frightened, as has been noted about *Resident Evil.* In Silent Hill, the gamer is in a continuous state of dread. On the other hand, if feeling fear—as intensely and as abundantly as possible (as Tan would say)—is the core of survival horror, the study of emotions created by *Silent Hill* goes beyond the simple question of being scared.

In *The Philosophy of Horror or Paradoxes of the Heart,* Noël Carroll calls "art-horror" the fear and disgust that horror narratives and images are designed to elicit from the audience (1990, 24).[19] Cross-mediatic and fictitious by nature, and describing the response to impure monsters, art-horror is an occurrent emotional state (rather than a dispositional one such as undying envy) that has both a physical and cognitive dimension (1990, 24). Insofar as the etymology of the word "emotion" refers to the idea of "*moving* out," it involves the experience of a change of physical state, from a normal to an agitated one. For Carroll, art-horror implies a "feelings" mode. Its recurring feelings or automatic responses are, among other things, muscular contractions, tension, shuddering, recoiling, chilling, a reflexive apprehension, and perhaps involuntary screaming. There is no doubt that the confrontations with the monsters and the bosses of *Silent Hill* evoke a deeply felt physical agitation. You may abruptly jump out of your seat upon unexpectedly encountering Nurses when entering a room. Your respiration may increase as if you were the one moving quickly while fighting Dogs and Flying Reptiles. You may lean forward in your chair, press your R2 Button harder, and brandish your controller at arm's length. You may swing the upper part of your body as if you were dodging and responding. Then, when the monster is killed or you manage to flee, you may calm down. Focusing on occurrent encounters with supernatural monsters, Carroll's art-horror holds as true for *Resident Evil* as it does for its numerous clones; but it falls short of defining the overall emotional dimensions at play in Silent Hill. To explain this, we must revisit H. P. Lovecraft.

For the author of *The Call of Cthulhu* (1926) and *The Shadow Over Innsmouth* (1931), the supernatural literature that he refers to as "cosmic fear"[20] is not to be confounded with mere physical fear and the mundanely gruesome.

> The true weird tale has something more than a secret murder, bloody bones, or a sheeted form clanking chains according to rule. A certain atmosphere of breathless and unexplainable dread of outer, unknown forces must be present; and there must be a hint, expressed with a seriousness and portentousness becoming its subject, of that most terrible conception of the human brain—a malign and particular suspension or defeat of those fixed laws of Nature which are our only safeguard against the assaults of chaos and the daemons of unplumbed space. (1973, 15)

The horror of Lovecraft is undeniably more psychological or metaphysical than physical. The creation of a given sensation is the final criterion, namely "a profound sense of dread, and of contact with the unknown sphere and powers; a subtle attitude of awed listening, as if the beating of the black wings or the scratching of outside shapes and entities on the known universe's utmost rim" (1973, 15). With its religious cult trying to bring about the birth of an Old God to destroy the world so it may be born anew, the plot of *SH: Origins*, *SH1*, and *SH3* expresses the belief that forbidden knowledge could destroy the human race and that there are unknown forces beyond the realm of our universe, forces as equally fascinating as dangerous. The aerial views of *SH1* work on that impression. The views showing Harry in the first broken stairs on the right of the drawbridge seem to be god's eye point-of-views. The main characters of *SH: Origins*, *SH1*, *SH2*, and *SH3* are similar to the typical Lovecraftian protagonists. They are facing both a dark world that they are not certain they fully comprehend and horrors that take them to the far corners of their (our) imaginations, leaving them (us) in awe as we watch and listen.

Art-horror and cosmic fear can be seen as the two poles of creating fear. However, there is a more classical opposition that is relevant to recall. In "On the Supernatural in Poetry," Ann Radcliffe clarifies: "Terror and horror are opposites, the first expands the soul, and awakens the faculties to a high degree of life; the other contracts, freezes, and nearly annihilates them" (1826, 149). Although I do not want to delve into the notion of sublime that this distinction of Gothic literature naturally leads to, I do feel inclined to speak, to a certain extent, about the sense of transcendence in terror. Will Rockett defines it in *Devouring Whirlwind*: "to transcend is to pass over or to go beyond the limits of oneself and to feel that one is in communion with that which is distinctly 'other,' or outside oneself" (1988, 6). I must admit that at moments I experienced a sense of transcendence in *SH2*. Obviously there is a certain status given to terror over horror, and authors of fiction aim at producing this overwhelming feeling of fear. To state his case, Rockett quotes Stephen King in *Danse Macabre*: "I recognized terror as the finest emotion ... and so I will try to terrorize the reader. But if I find I cannot terrify him/her, I will try to horrify; and if I find I cannot horrify, I go for the gross out. I'm not proud" (qtd. in Rockett 1988, 45). What's more, "King considers the provoking of terror a major means of 'transcending' the normal institutional limitations of the common horror tale" (Rockett 1988, 45). But even if we do not subscribe to this position—horror regarded implicitly as an inferior notion—the comments Rockett makes about the difference between horror and terror remain very informative. Horror is compared to an almost physical loathing, and its cause is always external, perceptible, comprehensible, measurable, and apparently material, while terror is identified with the more imaginative and subtle anticipatory dread. "In fact, terror is always of the indeterminate and incomprehensible, of the unseen but sensed or suspected, or of the imperfectly seen" (Rockett 1988, 46). Terror engenders a wonder in the face of the inexplicable supernatural. "The most common time of terror ... is night, a great absence of light and therefore a great time of uncertainty" (1988, 100). Without day's light, certainty, and clear vision, there is no safe time; terror expands on a longer duration. But we should not place terror and horror in direct opposition, as the Gothic writers did. As Dani Cavallaro observes in *The Gothic Vision*: "Binary oppositions ... are ultimately bound to prove reductive rationalizations. What is ... proposed, in an attempt to avert the dangers implicit in binary thought, is that terror and horror are closely interconnected and that each is capable of metamorphosing into the other" (2002, 5). The truly scary stories actually go further.

> The interaction of terror and horror is most explicitly conveyed by stories that articulate the experience of fear as an ongoing condition. Such narratives intimate that fear is not triggered by a single disturbing moment or occurrence but is actually a permanent, albeit multi-faceted, aspect of being-in-the-world. Concrete and intangible phenomena contribute equally to its dynamics. We oscillate constantly between terror and horror because we may only endure the pervasiveness of fear to the extent that we may be willing to acquaint ourselves with its more or less subtle modulations and transformations. (Cavallaro 2002, 6)

Much as in the interaction between the bottom-up (data-driven) and top-down (concept-driven) processes in our perceptual and cognitive activity, where one process can dominate in a context,[21] terror or horror can come to dominate the emotional experience.

Admittedly, there are great moments of horror in *Silent Hill*, and the monsters encountered during the experiential route play an important role. But terror applies most entirely to the overall psychological approach and the emotional experience. Expanding on the elements of survival horror, we could employ Rockett's argument that *Silent Hill* "transcends" the limitations of the genre. The series opens up a new territory. It creates its own subgenre (in which the *Fatal Frame* series is to be included). In the final analysis, to demonstrate how it stands out in comparison to the majority of survival horror games, it would be more appropriate to refer to *Silent Hill* as a paradigm of *survival terror*.

CHAPTER 2

Characters' Nightmarish Delusions in a Resort Town

> So what exactly happened to *Silent Hill*? That resides inside your imagination, and that is the truth about what fell on *Silent Hill*.
> —SH1 *FAQ, Konami Tokyo official website*, 1999

Fiction Emotions

SH1 has been praised, not only for its new formal and gameplay features, but also for its story. As Pascal Luban points out in his article "Designing and Integrating Puzzles in Action-Adventure Games":

> [A] story is at the heart of any adventure game, but the kind of story we look for in a [mixed] game like *Silent Hill* stands out in a unique way: in classical adventure games and in action-oriented games, the player controls the world; in mixed games, the world controls the player; he becomes the object of the game. The dramatic intensity of the narration is much stronger. (2002)

There is a secret plot behind *Silent Hill*: to target you, the *intriguee*, and control the order and pace of your discoveries and encounters. In order to accomplish this, Team Silent sticks to a fairly linear adventure, as compared to a RPG like *Planescape Torment* (Black Isle Studios / Interplay, 1999) as demonstrated by Diane Carr (2006, 59–71). The map of the city is marked and literally shows you where to go next. Apart from scattered, succinct in-game information, the storytelling takes place primarily out-of-game in cut-scenes that introduce the principal characters and unfold the narrative. On the one hand, the cut-scenes take control of your player character away from you and are "user-unfriendly," as Richard Rouse characterized them (2001, 222).[1] On the other hand, they allow you to see the action without the stress of gaming. They (re)introduce what Tanya Krzywinska relevantly underlines as a fundamental pleasure of the horror film: losing control (2002, 215–16).[2]

Third-person story-driven games such as *Silent Hill* obviously create what Ed S. Tan calls "fiction emotions or F emotions." At the plot level (this is different at the gameplay level, which is the subject of chapter 4), gamers get as much pleasure as spectators, by being allowed to freely observe other people.

> The pleasure of observation and the pleasure of losing oneself in the fictional world may be considered two sides of the same coin. Viewers [and gamers] sojourn, in the imagination, in a fictional world where they run absolutely no risk; their fantasy is both encouraged and directed. The cognitive basis for this experience is the realization that one is in a fictional space. (Tan 1996, 33)

If the emotional experience originates from the fictional world and the concerns addressed by that world, it is also based on this safe involvement (no risk). Through the *diegetic effect,* that is, the illusion of being present in a fictional and virtual world, the gamer feels *as if* he were physically present in a real self-contained world that already exists before he gains access to it and *as if* he were witnessing the action taking place around him. But the gamer is in fact a "controlled witness" since the plot determines both the action taken by the characters and how this will be depicted. The notion of "interest" being the central emotional mechanism in such viewing, it keeps the gamer captivated through the plot.

> The narrative provides the clues for the future structure of the story. The better the clues are utilized, the more valuable the anticipated final situation. The more I do my best to follow the structure of the story, to anticipate new information, to link various facts, and to watch for irony or hidden meanings, the greater will be my long-term reward in terms of structural order. The same is true for the affective investment: the more I sympathize with the protagonist in all her trials, try to imagine what she is feeling, and give her my unconditional support, the greater my

enjoyment will be of the ultimate triumph, as well as of each little step that brings that triumph closer. (Tan 1996, 111)

If emotions can be characterized by an urge to act in a particular way until the episode is closed due to a change of situation (Tan 1996, 74–75), this action tendency—or tendency to establish, maintain, or disrupt a relationship with the environment—is only virtual at the plot level. You cannot grab a gun to defend the characters. You're forced to have an observational attitude in the noninteractive cut-scenes and in the various documents or notes you read. Fiction emotions emanate from the comparison of concentrated and magnified fictive events with the affective potential of comparable events in daily life. As Tan remarks:

> Most F emotions are empathetic because the action in the traditional feature film [and traditional action-adventure game] narration is realized by protagonists who display human traits and whose goals and fate are of interest to the film viewer [and gamer]. These include such emotions as hope and fear, anxiety, sympathy, pity, relief, gratitude, admiration, shame, anger, terror, joy, and sorrow. (1996, 82)

They are empathetic "to the extent that the significance that an event has for the character is part of the situational meaning structure" (1996, 174) for the gamer. There are also nonempathetic emotions, such as disgust and repulsion, for an action and all of the visual details that might accompany it.

Before paying special attention to the important empathetic emotions, I want to focus on the fictional world and then on the gamer's fictional emotions that are felt throughout the main story and especially when faced with monsters.

The Dark Side of a Resort Town

The town of Silent Hill is a main character in the series. As demonstrated in *The Making of Silent Hill 2* (Beuglet 2001), the designers were able to re-create the look of a small American town[3] using stills of real locations modeled into the game. Indeed, as the series composer Akira Yamaoka confesses, "The original *Silent Hill* was our attempt at making classic American horror through a Japanese filter" (Bettenhausen 2007a, 73; Yamaoka goes on to say, "And now with *SH5* [*Homecoming*, developed by Double Helix

Games], it's an American take on a Japanese-filtered American horror").[4] The town is described this way in a tourist pamphlet found by James (*SH2*) in apartment 104 of the Wood Side Apartments and also by Heather (*SH3*) in the Heaven's Night club (did James leave it there when he passed through the club with Maria?):

> Welcome to Silent Hill!
> Silent Hill, a quiet little lakeside resort town. We're happy to have you here. Row after row of quaint old houses, gorgeous mountain landscape, and a lake which shows different sides of its beauty with the passing of the day, from sunrise to late afternoons to sunset. Silent Hill will move you and fill you with a feeling of deep peace. I hope your time here will be pleasant and your memories will last forever. Editor: Roger Widmark.

The history of the town is recounted in a few documents found here and there. For instance, in the book entitled *Lost Memories* (found in a newspaper stand outside the Texxon Gas Station in *SH2*) you discover that previously "this town went by another name. But that name is now hopelessly lost in the veils of time. All we know is that there was another name, and that for some reason the town was once abandoned by its residents."[5] Later on, in 1880, the Brookhaven Hospital "was built in response to a great plague that followed a wave of immigration to this area" (memo at the hospital, *SH2*). Yet various pieces of information shade this factual history and the idealistic vision that James and Mary have of their "special place." For example, a locally published magazine that James comes across in an office of the Toluca Prison indicates:

> Toluca Lake, the town's main tourist attraction. This clear, beautiful lake has another side as well. It may seem like just a typical ghost story that you might find in any number of old towns across the country. But in this case, the legend is true. On a fog-bound November day in 1918, the Little Baroness, a ship filled with tourists, failed to return to port. A newspaper article from back then simply says "It most likely sunk for some reason." Despite an extensive police search, not a single fragment of the ship nor any of the 14 bodies of passengers or crew has ever been recovered to this day. In 1939, an even stranger incident occurred.
> (There are many pages torn out)
> Many corpses rest at the bottom of this lake. Their bony hands reach up towards the boats that pass overhead. Perhaps they reach for their comrades. (*SH2*)

Lisa Garland, the nurse, also explains to Harry in a cut-scene:

> Before this place was turned into a resort, the townspeople here were on the quiet side. Everyone followed some kind of queer religion; weird occult stuff, black magic, that kind of thing. As young people moved away, the people figured that they'd been summoned by the Gods. . . .
>
> When several people connected with developing the town died in accidents, people said it was a curse. (*SH1*)

There is obviously something wrong with Silent Hill. When Harry comes to town, his initial remark is, "It's strange. It's quiet. Too quiet. This place is like a ghost town" (*SH1*). The first person he meets, police officer Cybil Benet, reaffirms that "something bizarre is going on. . . . The phones are all dead, and the radio, too." The first person James meets before getting into Silent Hill, Angela Orosco, warns him: "I think you'd better stay away. This uh . . . this town . . . there's something . . . 'wrong' with it. It's kind of hard to explain, but . . . And it's not just the fog either . . . It's . . ." (*SH2*). On their way to find Claudia, Douglas the detective, not knowing that Heather was born and raised there, says, "That's one screwed up town" (*SH3*). Crossing Toluca Lake on a boat in order to get to Silent Hill and to the last part of the journey, Deputy Wheeler tells the player character Alex Shepherd and his childhood friend Elle Holloway that "this place has bad history. Always has" (*SH: Homecoming*).[6]

Masashi Tsuboyama's notion of "strangeness," as employed in his discussion regarding the general atmosphere of the games, is evoked upon the discovery of a town that has been completely deserted by its inhabitants (the normal ones in any case) and plunged into mist and darkness and where it's snowing out of season.[7] As opposed to the nightmarish side, you can feel frightened and stifled in the normal side of Silent Hill because you can compare the game situation with typical everyday experiences and then imagine what it might be like. Anyone who has woken up early and wandered through empty streets might remember the strange feeling. They might recall the sudden distress felt at an evening power failure that causes the house to fall into complete darkness. Anyone who has walked or driven into a thick fog may have felt alone and anxious about what could appear in his or her field of vision. We might all have made slow progress in badly lit corridors or space, or have navigated damp and gloomy concrete underpasses, either with or without dripping water. One may have visited or seen dilapidated abandoned buildings with torn wallpaper and broken ceramic tiles, and so on. Additionally, the fictional and virtual environment of the *Silent Hill* series exploits all the experiential potential of claustrophobic spaces. You always move downward and deeper underground or are flung into an abyss. You ride elevators down, use many tight, steep staircases, climb down many ladders, and jump into a few black holes. These descents lead to murky basements, creepy sewers, disorienting labyrinths and catacombs, an old prison built during the Civil War, or a deserted subway station; but most important of all: they lead to an Otherworld.

Many everyday places of Silent Hill are turned into a nightmarish world: the Midwich Elementary School (*SH1*), the Alchemilla (*SH1* and *SH: Origins*) and Brookhaven (*SH2* and *SH3*) hospitals, the shopping district area (*SH1*), the Lake View Hotel (*SH2*), the Riverside Motel (*SH: Origins*), the Central Square Shopping Center and the Hilltop Center (*SH3*, not in Silent Hill though), the Lakeside Amusement Park (*SH1* and *SH3*), the Artaud Theater (*SH: Origins*), and the church (*SH3*). During these sequences of delusion, art director Masahiro Ito and sound director Akira Yamaoka take advantage of all the traditional horror images and ambiences to create Tan's primary nonempathetic emotions, namely disgust and repulsion. You hear all kinds of industrial and creepy sounds. Streets or floors are replaced by rusty grates over a bottomless abyss and are full of holes (into which Heather can fall). Walls and floors are spattered with blood or covered with streaks of blood. They even bleed, swarm, and burn like glowing embers in real-time in *SH3*, for the first time in the video game industry, as Yukinori Ojina the program director asserts (in Beuglet 2003). Walls turn into rusty plates and fences or are padded as in a madhouse, while paint falls from them (as in *SH: Homecoming,* an effect inspired by the film). The rooms are wrecks. Chains are hanging from the ceiling in the elementary school. Classrooms are furnished with a few metal chairs and large tables. Sinks and toilets overflow with blood. Dolls and dead bodies are crucified on the walls. Objects are located in strange places, for instance, the broken wheelchair (seen throughout the series) that Harry finds for the first time in the lobby of the elementary school and the gurneys containing bloodstained corpses that Heather sees in the shopping mall. The most repulsive images are to be found in *SH3*: a particularly striking representation is the figure of a mother holding her baby with her womb cut open who is situated in the ECHO Interiors & Floor Fashions of the Hilltop Center (fig. 2).

One of the main features of gameplay is the navigation through space; therefore the attraction of a labyrinthine town is without doubt enormous.

Fig. 2. *Silent Hill 3:* A mother holding her baby with her womb cut open

However, the role of Silent Hill is even more important in the series. In interviews, Akihiro Imamura usually gives the same answer to this question:

> IGN: Have any films or filmmakers inspired the creepy atmosphere you're hoping to achieve with *Silent Hill 2*?
>
> IMAMURA: Certainly David Lynch. His style has influenced the series, especially *Silent Hill 2*. *Twin Peaks* is one of my personal favourites. (Keeling 2001)

Although he has moderated his preference for David Lynch by saying in an interview: "With *Silent Hill*, I usually mention his name since he is a popular director and is easy to relate to for the non-Japanese audience. But I am not particularly limiting myself to just his films" (Sato 2001). It is difficult to avoid a comparison with Lynch's work and his TV series *Twin Peaks* (1990–91). Twin Peaks is the name of a picturesque American town in the rural Northwest. Its peace and order are disrupted when the high-school homecoming queen, Laura Palmer, is murdered. The investigation FBI agent Dale Cooper conducts brings to light the fact that the inhabitants are not what they appear to be. The town is not as typical as it seems. Legends draw attention to other worlds where the spirits inhabit (the White and the Black Lodges). The inquiry finally reveals a supernatural evil spirit in the town, Bob, a parasite requiring a human host and feeding itself on fear and pleasures.[8] This quick summary outlines some of the similarities between the plots of *Silent Hill* and *Twin Peaks*. Lorenzo Bassanelli, the editor in chief of *Ps2Fantasy.com*, emphasizes the connection.

> I see *Twin Peaks* as the most important source of inspiration for *Silent Hill*—the setting, the fact that the city becomes a "metamorphic creature" mirroring the soul of the population of the town and . . . the fact that the whole story is after all a voyage of the "detective" towards insanity, self-destruction, "death." (Personal correspondence, 2003)

As the "Lost Memories" appendix of the Japanese version of *Silent Hill 3 Strategy Guide* states: "The town has indeed become a great catalyst for the manifestation of people's unconscious minds. It appears to have become a place that beckons to those who hold darkness in their hearts." Silent Hill is really a fictional environment, not only for the gamer but also for the characters themselves, characters that call into question the existence of the Otherworld and are not sure to grasp the status of the terrorizing worlds (real and unreal) surrounding them. As Imamura explains: "The town of Silent Hill has a mysterious force. It exerts influence on people, and the town shows a world which you cannot distinguish from nightmare or reality. Why does the town exert such force? No one has yet discovered the cause" (Davison 2001, 126). The ambiguity about what's happening in Silent Hill results in an opened space of understanding and interpretation.

A Play of Ratiocination

It is always amazing to think that some gamers (those who do not have to engage in "play research" as scholars) are reducing their free time of play in order to write walkthroughs for the benefit of others. But it is even more fascinating to realize that others are so passionate about games (*Resident Evil* at the front for survival horror) that they analyze and theorize about the plots. In regards to *Silent Hill,* I share the astonishment of Daragh Sankey in "Fear, Art and Silent Hill":

> The vagueness and ambiguity unsettles the player and adds to the tension, but it also means that a great deal of possible "readings" are possible with this game. While poring through long-forgotten Silent Hill fan sites, I came across some of the most outlandish interpretations of the game's meaning. I think it's incredible that console gamers could somehow be motivated to take flights of hermeneutical fancy normally reserved for scholars' analyses of *Finnegans Wake* or *Guernica*. (Sankey 2001)

Examples of such works are found at the Silent Hill Wiki[9] and in the lengthy and deep plot analyses of Dan Birlew, Duncan Bunce, and others.[10] And this is not to mention the numerous discussions in Silent Hill forums, with topics entitled "I think we've been going about this all wrong (SH's plot)," "About Alessa's father," "Is James real or is it all imagination?" "The town's metaphysics," "God is not Samael," "The theory to end all theories," and so on.[11] According to the quotation from the Konami website, which is used as an epigraph to this chapter, the games are definitely open to numerous theories and interpretations. Following Marc C. Santos and Sarah E. White in "Playing with Ourselves: A Psychoanalytic Investigation of *Resident Evil* and *Silent Hill*," such openness leads to a hermeneutic pleasure "based on our need to perceive things in terms of 'ordered' narration. As we experience a narrative's linear progression, we anticipate the unity of its conclusion—the tying together of its disparate lines. We experience hermeneutic pleasure as mysteries are solved and ambiguities clear up" (2005, 70). However, as soon as gamers recognize the complexity and depth of *Silent Hill*'s plots and start to reflect on them, like the aforementioned exegetes, their pleasures are not rooted as much in the stories themselves and the fate of characters who are struggling to understand both their past and what is happening to them, but in the narrative construction itself. Their emotions are not fictional but instead are based on the artifact (I'll address these type of emotions in the next chapter). Therefore, instead of exploring these interpretative avenues in detail again (the various theories can be researched easily on the Web), I would rather look at *Silent Hill* in light of Noël Carroll's thoughts about the horror genre in his seminal book *The Philosophy of Horror or Paradoxes of the Heart*. These ideas are strikingly useful in explaining the ins and outs of the genre while linking to the analysis I wish to make.

As the philosopher Mark Vorobej underlines in "Monsters and the Paradox of Horror," Carroll's curiosity theory has often been criticized for good reasons, particularly because it does not conceptualize fear as the core of horror. However, in his discussion of the fact that Carroll only takes into account cognitive engagement, Vorobej has foreshadowed an important developmental consideration in his emphasis on the imaginative dimension of horror fiction: "The curiosity theory yet may survive . . . in some mutated form by locating the central source of pleasure in our imaginative speculations about what monsters might be like. . . . Horror monsters exist, in large measure, in order to be destroyed" (1997, 238). Survival horror and terror games such as *Silent Hill* represent, precisely, this mutated form.

Carroll's account of horror involves essential reference to an entity: the monster. The art-horror he describes is a reaction to monsters. Monsters are defined "as abnormal, as a disturbance of the natural order" (1990, 15), "as unclean and disgusting" (21), as "any being not believed to exist now according to contemporary science" (27). Essentially, horrific monsters have two characteristics (42–43).

First, they are threatening. They are dangerous in two ways: (1) physically by being lethal or by their power to maim, and (2) psychologically by destroying one's identity, morally by seeking to destroy moral order, or socially by trying to advance an alternative society—this way is the icing on the cake, says Carroll. The monsters of *Silent Hill* (like all survival horror monsters) are meant to be frightening. They execute many lethal and maiming actions. Alone or in groups, they jump on you, lunge at you, make you fall on the ground, hit you, bite you, grab you, hang you, eat you, stab you, sting you, choke you, shoot you, spit at you, fire at you, shoot lightning strikes at you, and so on. As noted in chapter 1, witnessing these attacks is enhanced by the third-person perspective. With the exception of the accidental moves in *SH3*, which can periodically cause Heather to fall off an edge or drop into a hole, it's the monsters' attack that ends the game. While inhabiting Silent Hill and seeking out player characters (this is not a *Myst*-like world), the challenge is to survive these monsters. Although you can run away from many of them, you cannot escape the boss monsters—you cannot if you wish to carry on your quest and continue to fall into the abyss of the player characters' tortured souls. Unlike fiction where the question is "whether the creature can be destroyed" (Carroll 1990, 182), the player characters absolutely must destroy them or, for the Pyramid Head(s) of *SH2*, hold out long enough to make them kill themselves.

Second, the monsters are "impure," thus disgusting. Generated by an interstitiality, that is, a conflict between two or more standing cultural categories, the creatures transgress distinctions such as inside/outside, living/dead, insect/human, flesh/machine, and animate/inanimate. Beings that are already potentially disturbing, they can also be further exaggerated, as is the case of the giants roaches in *SH2* or the swarms of *SH: Homecoming*. The monsters of *Silent Hill* display a high degree of impurity. In *SH1* they transgress, in a way that is still classical, the living/dead and beast/human categories. Many bosses are magnified and impure insects; this is the case of Amnion, the final one of *SH: Homecoming*. But to our delight, we must admit that they have evolved away from the typical monsters. Imamura remarks:

> The reason why the designs of the monsters are different between *Silent Hill 1* and *2* is that in the first version they were made to reflect the psyche of a sick little girl, so I made the monsters as symbolic butterflies and destructive bugs. For the second game, they are a reflection of one man's insane, twisted mentality. (Mackman 2001)

Masahiro Ito, the designer of the monsters in *SH1*, *SH2*, and *SH3*, has found a perfect way to disgust you: "Ito's secret is that he refuses to use elements that are too far removed from the human being. His monsters don't have horns or tentacles; their weapons consist only of deformed human appendages. Here, a head that attacks. There, swollen heavy arms" (Beuglet 2003).[12] The mutations of *SH2* and *SH3* do not lead to biotech monstrosities or call upon old demons. They bring out grotesque horrible humanoid creatures, yet not quite the classical zombies. In keeping with the medical origins of the delusions,[13] the majority of the foes look like they are disabled beings. They transgress categorical distinctions, but if they have some originality, it's because their main interstitiality is between the unborn and the dead. As much as they might look like they are already dead (for example, the Insane Cancers of *SH3* with their soured flesh and the Smogs of *SH: Homecoming* with tumors sprouting all over their body), they simultaneously appear to have been born at a very early embryonic stage. They do not have faces yet (not even the Nurses); parts of their bodies like arms and hands are not formed (the Patient Demons in flesh straitjackets of *SH2* and *SH: Origins*, the Numb Bodies of *SH3*); they have various malformations and deformities (the Underhangers of *SH2*, the Closers and Slurpers of *SH3*); their walk is dubious; and so on.

These two monsters' characteristics enable the horror genre to elicit the proper emotions. In a subsequent essay about film where he compares the emotional response to suspense, horror, and melodrama, Carroll comes to this conclusion:

> The horror analyst will attend to the way in which the monster is structured to bring properties in accordance with the criteria of harm and impurity to the fore, and to the way the plot affords opportunities both to allow the monster to display these properties and to permit human characters an occasion to talk about and to describe them. (1999, 46)

At one point, the characters of *Silent Hill* effectively end up questioning both the nature and presence of the monsters. Upon Harry's arrival at the examination room of the Alchemilla Hospital in *SH1*, Dr. Michael Kaufman wonders about the Flying Reptile that had made its way inside and that he has just killed. He says: "Something's gone seriously wrong. Did you see those monsters? Have you ever seen such aberrations? Ever even heard of such things? You and I both know, creatures like that don't exist!" In *SH2*, James often makes quick references to the monsters and even asks Eddie, during their first encounter, if he was a "friend with that red, pyramid thing." Sick on the floor, Eddie answers that he doesn't know what James is talking about, but says, "I did see some weird-lookin' monsters. They scared the hell outta me." The monsters are repulsive and generate nonempathetic emotions. Because their abnormality is linked to our human nature, they are in a good position to kindle our imaginative speculations. As Vorobej observes, "The true object of fascination in horror is *ourselves,* and the human condition in general. Battling monsters is a highly veiled odyssey of self-exploration. A monster's description must be significantly inchoate if each of us is to imprint his or her personal psychic concerns on the fiction" (1997, 239). The imprint has a particular overtone in *SH3* during a chat between Heather and Vincent, a priest of the Order, in the church's library:

> VINCENT: You're the worst person in this room. You come here and enjoy spilling their blood and listening to them cry out. You feel excited when you step on them, snuffing out their lives.
>
> HEATHER: Are you talking about the monsters?

VINCENT: Monsters . . . ? They look like monsters to you? (Heather grumbles.) Don't worry, it's just a joke.

The characters in *Silent Hill* certainly see the monsters from their own emotional and moral viewpoints.[14] The scenario writer Hiroyuki Owaku has commented, "Some philosophies explain that what you see is not necessarily reality. What you are seeing may not be what I'm seeing. The same is true of the monsters that you encounter in the game. . . . Maybe they are human beings just like you, maybe even your neighbors. What you see might be true or false" (in Beuglet 2003). This duality always introduces a certain amount of doubt about what is being seen, as well as some bewilderment regarding the "undeniable 'kill to survive' motivation" at the core of horror games (as noted by Rouse [2009], quoted in the previous chapter).

As important as it may seem, the monster does not exist for its own sake. The paradox of horror, is for Carroll, sorted out this way: "In order to account for the interest we take in and the pleasure we take from horror, we may hypothesize that, in the main, the locus of our gratification is not the monster as such but the whole narrative structure in which the presentation of the monster is staged" (1990, 181). Although curiosity drives most narratives, the horror story is explicitly driven by it "because it has at the center of it something which is in principle *unknowable*" (182). Knowledge and discovery are important themes, and suspense a key narrative element. "Most horror stories, including the most distinguished ones, tend to be elaborated in such way that the discovery of the unknown (voluntarily or otherwise), the play of ratiocination, and the drama of proof are sustaining sources of narrative pleasure in the horror genre" (126). Therefore, Carroll states, "The disgust that [the horrific monsters] evince might be seen as part of the price to be paid for the pleasure of their disclosure" (184). To reiterate, his curiosity theory has been discussed comprehensively; but in regard to survival horror and *Silent Hill*, his comments may be viewed in a new light.

To begin with, and it is the most obvious change that needs to be underlined at once, the video game literally involves a cognitive engagement, a play of ratiocination. At the gameplay level, the incursion of the monsters into the world of the characters serves, again referring to Vorobej (1997, 225), as a catalyst for challenging exercises in decision making, reasoning, and problem solving. While they get your adrenaline pumping, and place the lives of the player characters you control in the game world in peril, the monsters make the experiential route of fear more difficult since the exploratory narrative structure of games requires you to walk through the terrifying world and to search and locate hints in order to reach different places where the story will be progressing. Carroll talks about the "drama of corridors" (1990, 38), and this expression applies quite well to the maze structure of adventure video games and, referring to Henry Jenkins's "Game Design as Narrative Architecture," to the "pre-structured but embedded within the mise-en-scene awaiting discovery" (Jenkins 2004, 126). As Ewan Kirkland demonstrates in "Storytelling in Survival Horror Video Games" using as an example the *SH: Origins*'s level at the Cedar Grove Sanitarium (2009, 68), the stories of *Silent Hill* and of horror games really have to be reconstructed from scattered narrative information and brief encounters or events. However, inasmuch as we may agree with Vorobej when he asserts that "the play of ratiocination within horror rarely becomes that innovative, complex, or abstract" (1997, 235), we must also recognize that the *Silent Hill* series is an exception; *SH: Origins*, *SH1*, and *SH3* form a whole consisting of interconnected parts.

The Tortured Soul(s)

SH: Origins begins on a road at night when the trucker Travis Grady—the player character—takes a shortcut past Silent Hill in order to get to Brahms in time. When he sees a figure suddenly emerge on the road, he brakes and immobilizes his truck to look for it. He doesn't find it, but he does see the reflection of young girl in his truck mirror. Subsequently the girl, Alessa Gillespie, appears before him for the sole purpose of dragging him out to her burning house just in time to rescue her. Travis collapses after his heroic action, only to awaken later on a street bench in the foggy town. From this point onward, the play of ratiocination of *SH: Origins* is about the destiny of those two characters, currently linked to one another.

By going off in search of the burned child, Travis uncovers his tragic past. During his lengthy exploration of the Cedar Grove Sanitarium, he discovers that his mother, Helen Grady, has been incarcerated in the sanitarium. She had tried to kill him when he was young because, as she says in an audiotape reel, the "people in the mirrors . . . saw the devil inside of him."[15] It is further revealed, in an incident report found in the Storage Room, that the young Travis had attempted to enter the sanitarium to see his mom, but was taken by his dad. When he reaches the Riverside Motel, the place is somewhat familiar to him because when he was young he had sojourned there with his father (while visiting his mother, we can infer). As a matter of fact, Richard Grady committed suicide (a result of depression) in Room 503 of the motel and was found by Travis. Similar to the earlier moment when Travis is going to see his "momma" (one of the bosses like his father), the discovery of the suicide is shown in a flashback—or a delusion. It elicits fiction emotions related to a boy's heartbreaking childhood. This is obviously also true for Alessa, as her childhood elicits similar fiction emotions.

As a prequel, *SH: Origins* presents the first stage of the subsequent events and introduces supporting characters like Dr. Kaufman and nurse Lisa Garland. If Travis rescues Alessa from the fire, he doesn't necessarily save her from the Order, which is the religious cult that her mother Dahlia Gillespie belongs to. Dahlia attempted to burn her child to give birth to a new God (the mother is seen at the beginning while the house is in fire). Alessa's tortured soul uses Travis as a "pawn"—as Dr. Kaufman phrases it at the end— to find the five different pieces (Future, Past, Falsehood, Truth, and Present) of the Flauros. The Flauros is a pyramidal device that provides the "ability to control and amplify thought" and is considered to be "a weapon left by angels as a force of good" (according to a yellowed page found at the Green Lion Antique Shop). In order to accomplish this goal, Alessa allows Travis to cross to the Otherworld through mirrors, lets him fight his demons to get the first four pieces of the Flauros in the Halo of the Sun (the cult's official seal), appears to him as an innocent little girl, and then brings him back to the misty world by wailing the now famous siren call that makes him fall unconscious (as Harry will also do in *SH1*). In fact, as Dahlia tells Travis in the Cedar Grove Sanitarium, he should not have trusted Alessa, who is supposedly dead according to the nurse, Lisa Garland. Because she brings into play the Flauros to liberate her power over the town, Silent Hill is transformed into the Otherworld. Alessa finally guides Travis to the location where the Order is conducting a ritual over her burned body, which is being kept alive. Travis at last faces, not a god, but the Demon contained in the Flauros. He enables Alessa to give birth to a newborn. In the Good Ending, after Travis gets back into his truck and leaves Silent Hill, we hear Harry Mason and his wife find the baby girl and say "Cheryl. We'll call her Cheryl."

SH1 starts like *SH: Origins*. Harry Manson is on his way to Silent Hill for a vacation, with his daughter Cheryl (his wife died of a disease that "has left a shadow over his shoulder"—manual). Harry sees a figure on the road. To avoid it, he swerves, consequently running his vehicle off the road. When he wakes up behind the wheel, his daughter is missing. Reaching town, he starts to follow a figure, which looks like Cheryl. *SH1*'s plot takes an important twist upon Dahlia Gillespie's entrance into the Silent Hill's Balkan Church. Harry is to follow the guidance of Dahlia that tells him he has to stay on a straight and narrow path. What looked like a simple quest to find his daughter in a ghost town turns out to be much more complicated. It becomes a drama of proof. Not only does Harry have to fight the monsters—and the town of Silent Hill can be seen as one of those—it's now necessary for him to identify where the horror comes from, and to demonstrate that there are more things on earth than the acknowledged ones. The terror will be long lasting due to the true evil spirit, who is not only physically threatening via her monstrous creations, but also (icing on the cake!) psychologically dangerous. For Harry (you), the play of ratiocination is quite complex. Four main lines of approach have to be taken into account:

1. The identity of the young woman whom Harry saw and avoided on the road in the opening cut-scene at the start of the game. This encounter initiates the following events. He sees the figure again in the boiler room when he encounters trouble and then again when the Midwich Elementary School resumes normalcy. Going where Dahlia says to go, Harry also glimpses the figure entering the Antique Shop and then again leaving the roof of the Lighthouse. He also finds a picture of the young woman, Alessa, in a room in the hospital's secret basement.

2. The status of Harry's "living nightmare" (as Lisa Garland names it on their first encounter). Harry often asks if he's dreaming. He tries to make sense of it, but the world turns upside down when he has mysterious headaches and passes out (compared to *SH: Origins*, he does not control the moments when he goes to the Otherworld). It's like "some kind of hallucination," he says after the police officer Cybil Bennett reveals information about the drug trafficking (is he drugged after all?).

3. The evil presence in the town. On their first encounter, Dahlia Gillespie talks about a cage of peace, the Flauros, which can break through the walls of darkness, and counteract the wrath of the underworld. On their second meeting, she talks about the town being devoured by darkness, childish sleep talk, and the crest of Samael, which is evident all over town (the one Harry found the first

time in the school's courtyard). Later on, Lisa Garland reveals the existence of the cult in Silent Hill.

4. The drug market. In the Antique Shop, Cybil explains the "darkness devouring the town" by a reference to a drug trafficking. According to a note found in the police station, the drug is made of a plant peculiar to the region called "White Claudia." The investigation is stalled and the dealers are still at large (according to the newspaper in The Jack's Inn office).

One important key to the mystery is given to Harry on the bridge of Sandford Street in the resort area. The real world turns into the Otherworld, but "this time it feels different. Rather than shifting from reality to a nightmare, this is more like reality becoming a nightmare." Harry realizes that the whole town is invaded "by a world of someone's nightmarish delusions com[ing] to life," as he says to Cybil at the boathouse just before Dahlia Gillespie meets up with them. After Dahlia's speech about the end of the world, Harry still follows her instructions and finally gets a handle on the demon he was running after. The figure of the young woman is Alessa, Dahlia's own daughter who was burned in the house fire seven years ago. Yet it is also Cheryl, the second half of Alessa's soul. Dahlia untangles the enigma in the final scene:

> For the seven years following that terrible day, Alessa has been kept alive, suffering a fate worse than death. Alessa has been trapped in an endless nightmare from which she never wakens. He [our God] has been nurtured by that nightmare. Waiting for the day to be born. That day has finally come. The time is nigh. Everyone will be released from pain and suffering. Our salvation is at hand. This is the day of reckoning When all our sorrows will be washed away. When we return to the true paradise. My daughter will be the mother of God!

But everything doesn't go as planned. A god is born, but he kills Dahlia before Harry kills him (the final boss). In the Good Ending,[16] Alessa comes back to give yet another newborn to Harry, who then runs down the road into the night with the baby in his arms.

Ultimately, Dahlia Gillespie is in fact the real monster of *SH: Origins* and *SH1*, one who is both socially and morally dangerous. Her queer religion, it could be construed, has completely displaced the path to deliverance and salvation. To understand this, it is relevant to turn to Rockett:

The threats to survival, the things to be feared lurking just beyond the rim of firelight in the cave, are the first to be assigned First Causes—demonic ones. Only thereafter, when deliverance or survival is achieved, does one cast about for something to thank. One gives a name to this unseen First Cause of one's joy: that of the Deity. Later, this name is extended beyond the source of deliverance to the source of all goodness. (1988, 10)

What's more, there is a symbiosis between the demonic and the divine: "Without evil to be dreaded, then overcome, goodness would remain unrecognizable. In turn, the demonic requires the divine to explain why the triumph of the demonic in the affairs of men is not complete" (Rockett 1988, 10). Accordingly, Dahlia and the cult have completely mixed up this mutuality by trying to return to the true paradise through fear, hate, and an endless nightmare, by releasing everyone's pain and suffering by worshiping Samael, the Prince of the demons, the angel of death.[17] As for the ambiguity about the monsters ("They look like monsters to you?"), there also remains an ambivalence about this Supreme Being that is clearly introduced in *SH3* during the exchange, quoted earlier, between Heather and Vincent in the church's library:

HEATHER: Yeah, you're on Claudia's side.

VINCENT: I told you not to put me in the same category as that madwoman.

HEATHER: Well you're pretty loony yourself.

VINCENT: It's true that we believe in the same god, but I'm quite sane.

HEATHER: So why did you help me out then? Was that also part of trying to resurrect god?

VINCENT: It's not uncommon for people to worship the same god and still disagree.

HEATHER: "God"? Are you sure you don't mean "Devil"?

VINCENT: Whichever you like.

For that matter, the plot of *SH3* is based even more strongly on a wicked and contradictory fusion. The Good Ending of *SH1* is definitely the logical link between the two (I'll deal with *SH2* in a separate section).

Much more quickly, but exactly like the entrance of Dahlia Gillespie in *SH1,* the encounter of Heather Manson—the player character—with

Claudia Wolf (wasn't the hallucinogenic plant called "White Claudia"?) triggers the play of ratiocination in *SH3*. Claudia, speaking about the monsters, states that "they've come to witness the Beginning," "the rebirth of Paradise, despoiled by mankind." And about the heroine: "Don't you know? Your power is needed. . . . I am Claudia. . . . Remember me, and your true self as well. Also, that which you must become. The one who will lead us to Paradise with blood stained hands." Consequently, she puts five questions[18] to Heather (the gamer). Those questions revolve around Heather's identity and her perceptions: (1) What's going on with all those monsters around? (2) Are the sinister transformations of places and the occurrence of nightmarish events real or only a dream? (3) Who is Claudia, whom Heather should recall? (4) What "true self" does she have to remember? and (5) What does she have to become?

Heather discovers the first clue about who she is when, in the nightmarish Green Ridge Mental Health Clinic, she comes across a picture of herself with a note written on the back: "Find the Holy One. Kill her?" When she arrives home Heather discovers that it is not her who will be murdered but her father. This is portrayed through a very emotional cut-scene. Claudia had Heather's father killed for two reasons; first, for revenge because he took Heather away from them (the cult) 17 years ago and, second, to fill Heather's heart with hatred because she will give birth to a god and build an eternal Paradise. At this important turning point in the plot, you learn that her father is Harry Mason, the one who killed the god Dahlia Gillespie tried to summon. Heather is revealed to be the baby that Harry received from Alessa and subsequently fled town with. A return to Silent Hill then becomes inevitable. The drama of proof ends at a church. Heather finds the answers to her queries. She learns who Claudia is: a close friend of hers in the cult, with whom she played cards in her room and to whom she gave a sixth-birthday card, writing in it that she loved her as if she was her real sister. She truly confronts the reality that she was Alessa (and Cheryl), upon finding her dad's diary and her school desk. Being Alessa/Cheryl, she still has a god to give birth to. But as for *SH1*, everything doesn't go as planned. Following the Good Ending of *SH1*, the Normal Ending of *SH3* shows the death of Claudia and the killing of the god that has been nurtured with hate.

Scenario writers Hiroyuki Owaku (*SH1* and *SH3*) and Sam Barlow (*SH: Origins*) have crafted an intricate plot, a prime driving force for the gameplay. Even though many details of the play of ratiocination have here been left out, my intention was to demonstrate how the main story of the series keeps the gamer interested and intrigued until the end, and how it creates fiction emotions. This is, to a large part, accomplished via the relationships between the characters.

Involved in the Drama

The main protagonists of *Silent Hill* have drawn attention from reviewers and gamers on account of the fact that they are not the expected hero types found in many other games such as *Alone in the Dark, Resident Evil, Parasite Eve,* or *Onimusha: Warlords* (Flagship / Capcom 2001). In *SH: Origins,* Travis Grady is an ordinary trucker with a troubled past (manual). In *SH1*, Harry Mason is a thirty-two-year-old writer (manual) and "only a tourist," he says as he introduces himself to the police officer, Cybil.

> Perhaps what really makes the game [*SH1*] so believable is how incredibly ordinary the main character is and how realistic the town is. Harry is just an average guy. He can't aim a gun very well, he can't run that fast, and he reacts to situations in ways that you might react to them yourself. He pants heavily after running for a while, he occasionally trips, and during the remarkable Full Motion Animation sequences, his face displays some very distinct facial expressions. When Harry is wounded, the dual shock controller vibrates to simulate Harry's heartbeat. With this little trick at work, you'll feel like you ARE Harry. With all his little shortcomings and his humanitarian attitude, Harry is probably the easiest game character for people to identify with of all time. (Broas 1999)

In *SH3,* Heather is just an ordinary girl, with a bit of a sharp tongue and quick temper (manual) which set her apart from the more frail or innocent heroines of *Fatal Frame, Clock Tower 3,* or *Rule of Rose* (Punchline / SCEI 2006).

> She's not a cop or a special agent, not some oversexed cartoon, and certainly not much of a badass. Truth is, she looks pretty awkward and uncomfortable, especially the first time she holds a gun. The fact that a computer-generated character can actually look "awkward and uncomfortable" at all is some kind of tribute to the game's designers, whom from the beginning have made a point of giving us ever more human and believable heroes. It makes the ensuing darkness and horror all the

more threatening by contrast ... and creators Akira Yamaoka and Masahiro Ito damn well know it. (Hudak 2003)

The protagonists of *Silent Hill*'s main story are unquestionably not "super-powered avatars, spring loaded by uncanny fallout and armed to expiate" (Carr 2006, 71). As Broas's review maintains, this distinction certainly allows for a better identification with the protagonist. However, having followed Tan's and Carroll's theories, it is impossible not to put this notion into perspective, as succinct as it may be (since this is also the object of a large debate).[19] For both of them, one cannot talk about identification since the emotional state of the character and the viewer, or the gamer, is not identical. For Carroll, one "can assimilate the internal evaluation of the [horrific] situation without becoming, so to speak, possessed by [the protagonist]" (1990, 95). In Tan's terms, "The situational meaning for the viewer [and the gamer] always contains, in addition to the situational meaning for the protagonist, an element of spectacle" (1996, 190). You can actively explore what it is like to be the protagonist in a particular situation, but you'll never be the protagonist. The exploration always depends upon your own experience. A gamer that has a young daughter may be more inclined to have a more comprehensive understanding of Harry's search for Cheryl and experience more intense fiction emotions. The notion of empathy refers to this activity. As Tan states, "Empathy calls up expectations about what a particular character is going to do and how he or she will react to events. These expectations are cognitive investments. Affective investments consist mainly of feelings of sympathy for the protagonist" (1996, 192). The action has to generate an increase in empathetic emotions, such as feeling fear *with* Travis, Harry, Heather, and James, rather than sympathetic emotional responses you may also feel fear *for* the protagonists.[20] To elicit the fiction emotions, *Silent Hill* confines its narration to only what the main protagonists know, that is, to the restricted narration so characteristic of investigation stories. With the exception of Cybil being attacked on her way to the amusement park, which is shown quickly, you follow Harry step by step in *SH1*. You do the same with Travis in *SH: Origins*. The only moment in *SH2* where James is not present is during the short conversation between Laura and Eddie at Pete's Bowl-O-Rama, which is not of great importance. *SH3* infringes upon this restriction by showing two important scenes Heather doesn't witness: (1) the conversation between Claudia and Vincent in the room at Jack's Inn (the conversation took place on Heather's arrival, which reveals that Vincent is lying to her); (2) the encounter between Claudia and Detective Cartland at the Lakeside Amusement Park where you learn that Claudia lied to the detective. Also, the final confrontation between Claudia and Vincent begins just prior to Heather's entrance. In this instance, you have more information than Heather and therefore may feel differently than she may be expected to feel.

While, Tan states, empathetic emotions may be complex, you are often made to empathize with a character by simply seeing what he or she is seeing. You do not always have to delve into the innermost feelings of the characters (1996, 198). Nevertheless, *Silent Hill* prompts the gamer to do this. Because both the perceptions and the sanity of the protagonist you control are uncertain, the psychological dimension runs much deeper than the empathetic fears created by the frightening atmosphere. When Travis regains consciousness in the lobby of the Alchemilla Hospital and meets the nurse, Lisa, who finds him to be a bit shaken up, Travis says the fire might have boiled his brain a little. As for Harry, he wakes up twice in the beginning of *SH1*, first in his car after the crash where he finds out Cheryl has disappeared, then in the Cafe 5to2 after he is killed by monsters in the narrow alley where, strangely, it gets dark. These awakenings blur the limits between what's real and what's not, and they have to be explained by a detour that cannot be ignored. As Takayoshi Sato, character designer and CGI creator for *SH1* and *SH2*, observes:

> Most people working for game companies are game freaks, but the *Silent Hill* team are artists and programmers first—mainly artists. *Silent Hill 2* is not a typical game because most of our staff didn't grow up playing games. Because of this, we hope to provide the gamer with a different sort of game. (Perry 2001b)

In interviews, Team Silent made more references to movies than to games. Of those references, one film is fundamental: *Jacob's Ladder*.

Adrian Lyne's movie (1990) tells the story of Jacob (Tim Robbins), an American soldier who is returning from Vietnam after a shocking battle experience. His life becomes a nightmare when the subway, and later a car, almost runs over him, when faceless humanoid creatures (resembling those found in *Silent Hill*) pursue him, and when his doctor and a brother in arms are killed. After various delirious states and dreams within dreams, he suspects that he has been used as a military guinea pig, a human subject in an army experiment. Upon this assumption, he attempts to discover the truth. He finds out about a drug called "the Ladder" that increases aggressive tendencies, which was tested on his battalion. Eventually, the viewer learns in a final sudden twist that the whole film was a hallucination. Jacob had actually died on an operating table in Vietnam and had never returned home. Depending upon how the viewer reacts to this odd ending, *Jacob's Ladder* is either a great or a terrible film. Among the many reviews of the movie, Roger Ebert's is very enlightening:

> Making a chart of the real and the imagined is not the point of "Jacob's Ladder," anyway. This movie is the portrait of a mental state. . . . Most films tell stories. "Jacob's Ladder" undoubtedly contains a story, which can be extracted with a certain amount of thought. (Since the ending can be read in two different ways, however, the extraction process could result in two different stories). That isn't the point. What "Jacob's Ladder" really wants to do is to evoke the feeling of a psychological state in the audience. We are intended to feel what the hero feels. (Ebert 1990)

Allusions—and I'm aware that I'm one foot in the artifact territory dealt with in the next chapter, but it is important to understand the story—to *Jacob's Ladder* are inevitable when one talks about *SH1*. At one point, Harry asks himself in the hospital: "I don't want to think so, but maybe this is all just going on in my head. I could have had a car accident, and now I'm lying unconscious in a hospital bed. I don't know what's real anymore." What's more, this assertion becomes a premonition if you did not (1) obtain the red liquid that dispels evil spirits (the Aglaophotis) at the Alchemilla Hospital in order to save Cybil later, and (2) see Dr. Kaufmann at the motel in the resort area, while running by it too fast and going too far out on the bridge at Sandford Street, which results in the real world shifting to the Otherworld with no turning back. By missing the item and failing to engage in the action, you actually get an image of Harry unconscious or downright dead behind the wheel of his truck (the Bad Ending). As opposed to the basic narrative convention of the video game, the hero does not ultimately prevail.[21] If the various endings do matter, it is certainly because they allow different interpretations and give different shades and nuances to the game. But still, you empathize with Harry's disorientation throughout the game. With him, you come to question the reality of both the Otherworld and the real one. Given that there are monsters in the fog of Silent Hill, it is hard to trace a frontier between the known and the unknown. This is also true for *SH3* (I'll talk about *SH2* in the next section). Like *SH1*, the game begins with a longer nightmare, from which Heather supposedly wakes up. But again, given that the huge monster in her dream is found in "reality," there appears to be a breach there too. When Heather exits the elevator of the Central Square Shopping Center, which brings her to the Otherworld for the first time, she catches a glimpse of gory horror and asks herself: "Is this a dream? It's got to be. Not even a kid could believe in this. But when am I gonna wake up?" And yet, she has already woken up in the restaurant. During the next shift in reality (in the bathtub in one of the rooms in the ECHO Interiors & Floor Fashions), you hear a line from *SH1* spoken by her father, Harry Manson, who is explaining: "It's being invaded by the Otherworld. By a world of someone's delusions come to life." Does Heather hear this voice while she is fainting after succumbing to the pain of her throbbing head? If so, this is a hint about her being Alessa, or like Alessa. Consequently, she is the origin of the Otherworld, a situation that the Possessed Ending brings out better since it reveals that Heather has killed the detective, Cartland. But at the same time, she is also responsible for the vision of the real world. In this perspective, it is not possible to neglect the reference to David Lynch. As Bassanelli from *Ps2Fantasy.com* summarizes:

> Like Lynch, the authors of *Silent Hill* see external reality as a mirror of our souls, an extension of the character/individual's inner life. Imagination is reality (also to quote the recent Bellocchio movie *Good Morning, Night*, 2003), and flows of time and space are variable according to our inner feelings, thoughts, rhythm; truth is always relative, the boundaries between life and death, between sanity and insanity are difficult, if not impossible, to define. (Personal correspondence, 2003)

H. P. Lovecraft has made Jervas Dudley, the narrator of *The Tomb* (1917), profess the same opinion while extending the scope:

> It is an unfortunate fact that the bulk of humanity is too limited in its mental vision to weigh with patience and intelligence those isolated phenomena, seen and felt only by a psychologically sensitive few, which lie outside its common experience. Men of broader intellect know that there is no sharp distinction betwixt the real and the unreal; that all things appear as they do only by virtue of the delicate individual physical and mental media through which we are made conscious of them; but the prosaic materialism of the majority condemns as madness the flashes of supersight which penetrate the common veil of obvious empiricism. (Lovecraft 1970, 7)

Even a doctor's journal, found by James in the document room of the Brookhaven Hospital of *SH2*, acknowledges the interconnection:

> The potential for this illness exists in all people and under the right circumstances, any man or woman would be driven like him, to "the other side." The "other side" perhaps may not be the best way to phrase it. After all, there is no wall between here and there. It lies on the borders where reality and unreality intersect. It's a place both close and distinct. Some say it isn't even an illness, I cannot agree with them. I'm a doctor, not a philosopher or even a psychiatrist.

As much as *Silent Hill* isn't just a game series but an emotional experience, Lynch's work suggests that *Lost Highway* (1997) and *Mulholland Dr.* (2001) aren't just movies but surrealistic experiences, and most viewers would concur. In both cases, it is a portrait of a mental state. It is a play *of* the mind, a play *with* the mind.

If the experience of *Silent Hill* is lived through ordinary but endearing player characters, the NPCs are not to be cast aside. Team Silent has complied with a precept of game design that Richard Rouse in *Game Design: Theory & Practice* and Pascal Luban in "Turning a Linear Story into a Game" put forward:

> Instead of trying to imbue the main character with a lot of personality, make the NPCs the player encounters in the game memorable and interesting. If the player finds these characters annoying that is totally acceptable; it means that they have enough personality for the player to feel strongly about them. (Rouse 2001, 230)[22]

> Pay great attention to secondary characters. They have a critical function in a story. They supply motivation to the hero, bring personality and life to the world created by the author and are often the best way to introduce new developments. In terms of gameplay, these characters also lend themselves to multiple uses: they may help the player by guiding him across a maze or fighting by his side ... or may die for the player so that our hero can stay alive and well. (Luban 2001)

The NPCs of *Silent Hill* are simultaneously intriguing and disturbing. As is exemplified by Alessa Gillespie, who was the most important NPC, they reveal their true personalities during the course of the various encounters with the main protagonists.

In the enemy camp, the blind beliefs of Dahlia Gillespie (*SH: Origins* and

SH1) and Claudia Wolf (*SH3*) in the Order really make them wicked characters. Mysterious, yet elusive and manipulative, they respectively advise Travis, Harry, and Heather, both for their own benefit and for the good of their religious cult. Consequently, they follow the path that becomes their fate, which according to Dahlia has been foretold by Gyromancy. If Dr. Kaufmann remains the typical unpleasant bad guy (*SH: Origins* and *SH1*), Vincent (*SH3*) is difficult to figure out. As demonstrated by the chat previously transcribed, you never know where you stand with this priest of the Order. He is funny, yet mischievous. It is difficult not to have misgivings about the advice he gives to Heather.

In the collaborator camp, the female police officer Cybil Bennett (*SH1*) from Brahms (Deputy Wheeler talks about her disappearance to Alex and Elle in *SH: Homecoming*) is the archetypal strong woman and ally for Harry. Therefore, she can only be expected to turn against him once she is possessed at the Lakeside Amusement Park. The nurse Lisa Garland (*SH: Origins* and *SH1*), who took care of Alessa, makes a much more moving appearance. When she introduces herself as a trainee to Travis, she shows both an innocent side and an alluring one. If she demonstrates her come-hither side at the Artaud Theater and only flirts with the trucker in order to show how she can act and "could be a star," she seems to have been more serious with Dr. Kaufmann in the motel room where Travis finds them. It is in the Otherworld that Lisa is more vulnerable. She is crying as Travis meets her in the Cedar Grove Sanitarium. In *SH1*, she takes refuge in Harry's arms immediately upon their first encounter (short prerendered cut-scene) when he finds her in the examination room of the nightmarish Alchemilla Hospital. She's confused and doesn't know what's happening. She provides in subsequent encounters important information about Dahlia Gillespie and Silent Hill's history, as well as finding a way to get to the lake. She is cold, does not want to be alone, but feels she cannot leave the place. In their last encounter in the "Nowhere" basement, Lisa has realized that if she is still alive, it's because she's one of them. At this moment, blood pours down her forehead and she starts to totter toward Harry. You sympathize for Lisa, but Harry must leave both the room and the nurse behind. *SH3* stages an even more sad moment. This time, it deeply touches the player character. It has been mentioned previously that she has only journeyed home in order to find her father, Harry Mason, who was murdered by Claudia's missionary. The loss is grievous, especially since Heather is not able to give her father a decent burial. With the help of Detective Cartland, she abandons her father under a white bedsheet in his room. Cartland is in some ways replacing Harry from now on. He is a nice guy and he listens to Heather with compassion on their way to Silent Hill. Wounded at the Lakeside Amusement Park, he confesses that Heather reminds him of his son, who was shot in a bank robbery. Although he points his gun at her because her death might be a way to end the nightmare, he doesn't shoot. The loving relationship that unites Heather and Cartland gives more scope to the Normal Ending, where she jokes with him and, above all, to the Possessed Ending. It is striking to find out that Cartland has been bloodily stabbed by Heather.

While the gameplay in *Silent Hill* is almost entirely based upon fear and terror, the encounters and relationships with NPCs, which are developed in cut-scenes, have to be credited for creating fiction emotions such as resentment, anger, pity, sadness, and sorrow.

Unreliable Psychological Journey

Despite the fact that it supplies additional information about the town of Silent Hill, the first reason to talk about *SH2* independently is that its plot is autonomous with respect to *SH: Origins*, *SH1*, and *SH3*. But the real motive is that *SH2* is a masterpiece that needs to stand out. It is psychological horror at its highest level, and psychological drama at its best.

Talking about the original aspects of *SH1*, Daragh Sankey notes that Harry Mason becomes an unreliable character since, as we saw earlier, he wakes up after death and blacks out periodically. "Thus the game's 'point of view'—in this case that of the third-person camera, which we generally trust to be impartial and objective—is rendered untrustworthy" (Sankey 2001). *SH2* plays upon this unreliability to an even greater extent. Unless you have finished the game once and got the "In Water" Ending, in which James gets into a car to kill himself in order to be with Mary, there is no hint (as there was in *SH: Origins*, *SH1*, or *SH3*) about the ambiguity of the reality you see; nor is there any indication of James Sunderland's insanity. He remains a protagonist whose age and occupation are unknown (manual). *SH2* starts with James pensive, but wide awake in front of a restroom mirror. From the outset the game is a drama of proof. James wonders whether it's possible that his wife Mary, who died three years ago from a damnable disease, wrote the letter he just received, a letter that leaves him unbalanced. He goes to Silent Hill hoping to establish that she's really alive and waiting for him. The first living being he encounters when he gets to town (after a talk with Angela at the cemetery) is a monster he has to kill. The first human he comes across is a dead man. On a memo page discovered near the corpse, James reads:

> I saw those demons. They were there, I'm certain. But my friend says he didn't see anything. If that's true, does that mean that what I saw was an illusion? But whether that demon that hates human beings was real, or whether it was just some kind of hallucination that my mind dreamed up ... one thing, I know for sure is that I'm beyond all hope.

While this memo talks about perception and hallucination, it nevertheless states a terrifying reality independent of James, therefore presenting his point of view as impartial and objective, to repeat Sankey's terms. Nothing yet allows you to tell that Silent Hill has called him on, that the experiential route is his own nightmarish delusions and that the monsters are a projection of his psychological state.

Once again, what looks like another quest to meet a loved one in a menacing city crawling with monsters turns out to be much more complicated. Although the play of ratiocination is theoretically meant to revolve around the search for the supposedly dead but possibly still alive Mary, it slowly strays toward another question.

> Scarier than any horror movie released in the last five years, *Silent Hill 2* works because you are the protagonist ... and yet, you aren't. Gamers can fully identify with the protagonist to the point where, like James, they're fearful of what new rooms and buildings hold—and simultaneously at enough of a remove to where it's clear to them that not everything is right with James' mind. (Maragos 2001)

SH2 expands on the distinction between identification and empathy. Whereas you empathize with James, you cannot identify with him, as you are missing an important piece of information. The secret of *SH2*'s plot (taken here both as the story line of the game and the conspiracy of the game designers) is doubly astonishing: (1) You reach the "special place" only to discover that James has killed Mary by smothering her with a pillow. As a result, the impulses of the soul are completely reversed. James did not enter Silent Hill to reach Mary, but rather to run away from his own act. It was not as much a matter of getting in as of getting out (Travis's stop is similar because his motivation is to leave a troubled past behind). The scene where James realizes his act is certainly one of the saddest moments of the survival horror genre. (2) As Krzywinska has noticed, *SH2* "attempt[s] to disrupt the conventional good/evil paradigm. This is achieved by building questions about the 'good' status of the avatar" (2002, 222 n. 3). Indeed, while a great majority of survival horror games present their heroes in roles of force and as maintaining the social order, in this case you've been empathizing and sympathizing with someone whose sickness pushed him to commit the murder of his beloved.

The devious plot of *SH2* undoubtedly has something to do with Agatha Christie's famous novel *The Murder of Roger Ackroyd* (1927). The character who narrates the story and assists Hercule Poirot in his investigation, Dr. Sheppard, is in the end the murderer the inspector is looking for. On the other hand, keeping within contemporary film references, the analogy made with *The Sixth Sense* (Night Shyamalan, 1999) sheds a great deal of light on the game. In this ghost story, Dr. Malcolm Crowe (Bruce Willis) is shot at the beginning of the film by a former patient he didn't help sufficiently. The story picks up next fall when Crowe is treating a young boy named Cole (Haley Joel Osment). Cole sees dead people and is assaulted by them. In order to survive his "sixth sense," Crowe makes clear to Cole that he must not fear the dead ones but rather help them out. This arrangement enables Cole to live peacefully but also to reveal to Crowe his true nature: Crowe himself is a dead person, a ghost, since he never recovered from the initial shooting. To maintain the surprise until the end, the stratagem of *The Sixth Sense* is simple. It focuses the action on Cole's parapsychological faculties rather than on Crowe's condition and consciousness of it.[23]

SH2's plot plays the same narrative game, but without the prologue. It focuses you on the search for Mary rather than on the real nature of James and on his true quest for redemption. Before the viewing of Mary's murder, all the clues are there, more or less obvious, noticeable, and easy to find or see. Depending of your play of ratiocination, you'll experience different fiction emotions if you suspect that Silent Hill is mirroring James's tormented soul. For instance, the dress on the tailor's dummy, which is holding the flashlight in Room 205 of the Wood Side Apartments, is Mary's dress. Likewise, as the director Masashi Tsuboyama explains, the corpse you find in front of the television set in Room 208 "is James himself! Same face, same polygonal model structure. In fact, this is an image straight out of James' imagination" (Beuglet 2001). There is a message written on the map of Silent Hill that James takes before leaving the Brookhaven Hospital: "He who is not bold enough to be stared at from across the abyss is not bold enough to stare into himself. The truth can only be learned by marching forward." If James (re)visits Neely's Bar on his second way to Rosewater Park, there is a graffiti on the wall: "If you really want to see Mary, you should just die. But you might be heading to a different place than Mary, James." On the tombstones of three opened graves in the catacombs' graveyard, there are the names of Eddie Dombrowski, Angela Orosco, and James Sunderland. To go on, James has to jump in his own grave. And during the game, the letter he received from Mary will fade away.

Needless to say, it's through memorable encounters with NPCs that the hidden nature of the journey begins to be more explicitly uncovered. As for *SH: Origins*, *SH1*, and *SH3*, the NPCs elicit a wider range of emotions. Angela and Eddie, the two characters who have their opened graves with James, are quite confused. They are strange and very moody. Their behaviors indirectly reveal the true nature of James's own behavior. Both Angela and Eddie will die. When James comes across Angela with a knife in her hand in the Blue Creek Apartments, he tells her that there's always another way. She replies with a line that James contradicts: she insists that he is the same as her and that "it's easier just to run. Besides, it's what we deserve." From a newspaper article, which was found before a cut-scene in the Labyrinth where Angela is assaulted by a monster (a Doorman), we learn that she killed her violent, alcoholic father, who had abused her. Her reaction to James is fearful, and when he wants to touch her, Angela pulls herself together and shouts at him that she knows he is a liar. Mary was not ill; he just didn't want her around anymore. That line leaves James without a voice. But the sympathy you may have felt for Angela lasts until the end considering that she'll commit suicide in the hotel fire. As for Eddie, he is fat, ugly, disgusting, and arouses nonempathetic emotions. The first time James meets him at the Wood Side Apartments, he is vomiting into the toilet of a room where someone was killed. Indeed, a person's death isn't a big deal for Eddie, as he kills people, not monsters in Silent Hill. He actually turns into a boss before James reaches the Lake Side Hotel. By the time of the fight, when James preaches about not killing people, Eddie replies: "Don't get all holy on me, James. This town called you, too. You and me are the same. We're not like other people. Don't you know that?!" Having defeated his opponent, James grasps that he has just killed a human being and asks himself if Mary actually died three years ago. This question arises more directly during his encounter with Laura. This little girl, strangely enough, wanders alone safely in Silent Hill. Initially she is a real brat to James, dragging him into the hands of monsters (the Boss Hangers). Even so, she knew Mary and declares to him that he didn't love her anyway. Laura's words evoke explicit doubts about what's actually going on. When James meets her at the Brookhaven Hospital, she says that she was a friend of Mary's who she had met at the hospital last year (not three years ago). At the Lake View Hotel, Laura makes James read the letter that she received from Mary, a letter in which Mary declares that she loved her like her very own daughter, that she would have liked to adopt her and wishes her a happy eighth birthday. The thing is, Laura turned eight last week. Just before the final discovery, and in order to better prepare the twist in the action, this revelation prompts James to believe Mary could still be alive. As with James, Laura also arouses sympathy upon the cruel loss. However, in the same way she crossed Silent Hill without harm, she brings about a rather happy ending (the "Leave" one), walking through a graveyard followed by James.

Whatever happens, the character of Maria is the most important NPC, especially since she accompanies James for a part of the game. It is she, and not Mary, that James finds at the Rosewater Park. Maria looks exactly like Mary and "could be her twin." She's seductive and takes advantage of it. She pushes James far too often, for instance, wondering presumptuously if he loved Mary or hated her. He leaves her alone in a room of the Brookhaven Hospital, because she's coughing and wants rest, and she later moans that he should never leave her alone because he is supposed to take care of her. James won't be able to do so, and she'll be killed in a cut-scene before they leave the hospital. This moment brings fiction sadness since you cannot do anything to save Maria from Pyramid Head's great knife. But not everything is right with Maria (being the projection of James's mind). James runs into her again in a prison cell of the Labyrinth. She initially pretends to be Mary. Given the fact that she knows about a VHS tape James and Mary recorded back at the hotel, she could be Mary. Suddenly changing attitude, she finally admits that she is not, yet argues that she is real by touching him. To his great despair, James finds her dead and mutilated in another sorrowful cut-scene when he reaches the other side of the room. Maria will be killed one last time, by the hand of a Pyramid Head, during the course of the journey.

The main monster of *SH2* is indeed James's Nemesis; but compared to the Nemesis of *Resident Evil 3*, Pyramid Head is not as brutal and remains indestructible. James sees him for the first time in Room 307 of the Wood Side Apartments in what looks like a weird sex scene.[24] It is also Pyramid Head who kills Maria at the hospital. James has to survive until a final confrontation with two Pyramid Heads, who are executioners from the past, which he discovers in the Historical Society Museum (in the Bogeyman Ending of *SH: Homecoming*, Alex Shepherd becomes one of those Pyramid Heads). They make him realize his error. Falling on his knees upon Maria's execution, James observes: "I was weak. That's why I needed you ... Needed someone to punish me for my sins ... But that's all over now ... I know the truth ... Now it's time to end this."

The story finally reveals that it is due to sickness, grief, and despair that the real evil resides inside Mary and James. In the conversation heard in the last long corridor James crosses, Mary cries out: "I'm disgusting! I don't deserve flowers. Between the disease and the drugs, I look like a monster. Well what are you looking at? Get the hell out of here." And in the letter to James, she wrote:

> When I first learned that I was going to die, I just didn't want to accept it. I was so angry all the time and I struck out at everyone I loved most. Especially you, James. That's why I understand if you do hate me. But I want you to know this, James. I'll always love you. Even though our life together had to end like this, I still wouldn't trade it for the world. We had some wonderful years together.

James responded to Mary's desire to die, to end the pain. In turn, he confesses to her: "That's why I did it, honey. I just couldn't watch you suffer. No! That's not true ... You also said that you didn't want to die. The truth is I hated you. I wanted you out of the way. I wanted my life back."

We have to admit that "*Silent Hill 2* is a lot more than just a horror game, more a terrible love story" (Beuglet 2001). It is a real emotional experience. *SH2* remains the best game of the series and, as a story-driven one, a unique video game.

CHAPTER 3

Designers' Cinematic Depiction of a Game World

> Play has a tendency to be beautiful. It may be that this aesthetic factor is identical with the impulse to create orderly form, which animates play in all its aspects. The words we use to denote the elements of play belong for the most part to aesthetics, terms with which we try to describe the effects of beauty: tension, poise, balance, contrasts variation, solution, resolution, etc. Play casts a spell over us: it is "enchanting," "captivating."
>
> —*Johan Huizinga,* Homo Ludens

Artifact Emotions

When asked about what he was hoping to achieve with the release of *SH2,* Akihiro Imamura answered: "You know, in our daily lives we don't really feel much fear. It's not a common emotional state in day-to-day life. Our aim is to stimulate that emotion with *Silent Hill 2,* so we hope you enjoy that!" (Keeling 2001). This response brings to light an important paradox regarding horror fiction. You actually do not feel much fear in your daily life, nor fright, dread, disgust, or repulsion, because these are all negative emotions you wish to avoid. Fear, John Morreal observes, "is perhaps the most basic negative emotion, and at first glance one of the least likely to be enjoyed. To feel fear, many have claimed, we have to judge that we are in danger, and danger is disturbing" (1985, 96). As the reference to Carroll's art-horror emphasized in the previous chapter, fear has an important physical dimension. What might make fear potentially enjoyable rests on the excitement, the "rush" or the thrill that it can bring, and many put themselves in danger just for the pleasure of it. Adventure, thus says Morreal, is precisely the name used to define this situation. Yet, as he also notes (catching up with Tan's thought about the guided fantasy and closed episode quoted in the beginning of the third part of the introduction), enjoyable fear needs to stay within certain limits. As a more general principle, the overall control of the situation must be retained and conserved; when something has consequences, negative emotions can get too strong and you unpleasantly lose control;[1] or, when a fear is objectless, as an anxiety, you are unable to control it.

> Control is usually easiest to maintain when we are merely attending to something which has no practical consequence for us, as when we watch from a distance some event unrelated to us. Here our control requires our ability to pay attention when we want, to stop paying attention when we want, and to direct our attention to those features of the event that interest us. When we have the ability to start, stop, and direct the experience, we can enjoy a wide range of experiences, even "unpleasant" ones. (Morreal 1985, 97)

If you get too scared in *Silent Hill*, you can always turn off your PlayStation (and wait before going to bed). But what makes a big difference in fiction, such as in the survival horror genre, is that you know that someone has created the situation you are responding to. In Carroll's view, this knowledge mutes the disturbing aspect of the object of art-horror and allows opportunity for fascination (1990, 189). Marcia Eaton asserts that "control permits us to attend to properties which provide us with aesthetic delight . . . , features [of a situation] which we would be unable to attend or to which it would be inappropriate to attend if we (or others) were genuinely endangered" (1982, 61).[2] For example, you can be surprised by the attack of a Nurse upon your entrance into a room of Silent Hill's hospitals and still notice how good the camera position is in that room.

The focus on the aesthetic experience bears relation to what Tan has, in this instance, called "artefact emotions or A emotions."

> As soon as they [viewers and gamers] are aware, no matter how fleetingly, of the operation of that intelligence [the editorial intelligence at work behind the film or game] they are in that instant aware of the film [and the game] as artefact. In a general sense, it may be that the more

intense the emotion, the greater the likelihood the viewer [and gamer] will realize that this is a special experience and be aware of what he or she is seeing is indeed an artefact. It is interesting that, in that case, the emotion evoked by the situation in the fictional world is one element of the situational meaning, which results in an emotion that has the artefact as its object. (Tan 1996, 65)

The pleasure of Tan's "Emotion Machine" not only derives from the fictional world depicted, the characters' fate and the fiction emotions this is eliciting, but also from the formal characteristics of the medium. This second source of primary satisfaction derives from the construction and twists of the plot (in fact, as I have underlined, that's what I just did in part by making parallels with the plots of *Jacob's Ladder* and *The Sixth Sense*), the stylistic features, technical manipulations, and formal order provided by the artifact organization. Although the appreciation might depend on a certain competence, since film and video game buffs are more inclined to do so, various tours de force can make the awareness of the form more effective. Spectacular special effects and impressive photography or graphics and staging represent such an instance. At times, spectacle takes precedence over the dramatic and psychological developments. Furthermore, Tan says there are "traditional genres in which watching fictional events is the prime attraction, almost divorced from their significance for the characters." The major scenes of horror films, and survival horror games, "are more than anything else a feast for the eyes, although perhaps not to everyone's taste" (1996, 175).

Artifact emotions result from an awareness of the artistry of creation. The surface structure is grasped and appreciated in its own right without direct relation to what's happening in the fictional world. You enjoy not as much fear itself, as the way fear has been designed. The pleasure thus lies less in the *intra*textual links than in the *inter*textual connections between the Silent Hill series and different works of art. The games are without a doubt precisely or diffusely "inhabited" by other artifacts with which they "interact" through references, similitudes, and various influences.[3]

Full of Details

Reviews do not often compare *Silent Hill* with other games.[4] For the most part, *Resident Evil* and *Alone in the Dark* are the survival horror points of reference. In the marking out of the parallel worlds and the transition to an

Other one, few references are made to the Dark World of *Darkseed* (Cyberdreams / Cyberdreams, 1992) and the Spirit Realm of *Legacy of Kain: Soul Reaver* (Eidos Interactive / Crystal Dynamics, 1999). Instead, reviewers, and the creators themselves tend to draw more attention to horror literature and cinema when discussing the series outside its own parts. Readers of H. P. Lovecraft, Clive Barker, Dean Koontz, and, more often than not, Stephen King are said to find themselves right at home in the resort town. Moreover, one King story is effectively cited and is easy to guess: the short story *The Mist* (1980).[5] If Team Silent recognizes the influence of film directors such as David Cronenberg, David Fincher, Alfred Hitchcock, David Lynch, Stanley Kubrick, and even Andreï Tarkovski, reviewers refer more to specific films. In addition to *The Exorcist, Jacob's Ladder,* and *Twin Peaks,* which was already mentioned, *The Blair Witch Project* (Daniel Myrick and Eduardo Sánchez, 1999), *Eraserhead* (Lynch, 1977), *The Evil Dead* (Sam Raimi, 1980), *House on the Haunted Hill* (William Castle, 1969), *In the Mouth of Madness* (John Carpenter, 1995), *Lost Highway* (Lynch, 1997), *Rosemary's Baby* (Roman Polanski, 1968), *Se7en* (David Fincher, 1995), and *The Shining* (Stanley Kubrick, 1980) are among others that are often mentioned.

If these allusions express the mood, style, and the terrified excitement of *Silent Hill,* one parallel drawn in 2001 by a *Gamezone.com* review of *SH2* sets out an interesting point of comparison that cannot be overlooked: "It amazes me how close the game is [to] *Toy Story* and *A Bug's Life* in terms of computer generated imagery. Words can't even begin to describe *SH2*'s graphical prowess. For the first time in my life, I actually felt like I was controlling a movie" (Bedigian 2001). Contemporary cinema and the video game do share the same insatiable thirst for spectacular tours de force to blow away spectators and gamers. *Toy Story* (John Lasseter, 1995), the first feature film made entirely by computer, astonished people at the time of its release by its stupefying realistic animation. The visuals and sound of the early games of *Silent Hill* have amazed the gamer in a similar manner. But one wouldn't expect less to come from artifacts created in an industry based on fast-changing computer technology. Undeniably, video game history is peppered with technological innovations and continual groundbreaking computer-generated imagery that create artifact emotions. It is an argument defended by Andrew Mactavish in "Technological Pleasure":

> I contend that a significant and relatively unexplored component of the pleasure of computer gameplay is our astonishment at visual and audi-

tory technology, at our participation in technological spectacle, and in the story of its development. In doing so, I describe the ways in which game designers use visual and auditory display to immerse players into a frenetic virtual world but also to draw attention to the game's virtual world as *virtual*. (2002, 34)

To make such claim, Mactavish points to Tom Gunning's notion of early "cinema of attractions," a cinema where the spectacle is based on direct confrontation and stimulation of the spectator's curiosity rather than on the creation of an utterly captivating, totally seamless narrative.[6] Mactavish also states that the pleasure of the video game is "a pleasure of accessing, witnessing and performing technologically mediated environments" (2002, 46), environments which are indeed increasingly realistic. As Ruth Amossy underlines, this pleasure is rather crucial for the industrialization of fear:

In a word, all techniques of presentation which are capable of provoking a surprise, a sudden chill that ably paralyzes critical abilities on the moment, confer to the stereotype of fear its effectiveness. From this comes the relatively brief existence of terror narratives and their rapid aging. The topicality of techniques of fear is extremely limited: effects are valid only for their novelty and their immediacy. This is why the industry of terror, where cinema occupies a preponderant place, works essentially to invent and to perfect its effects. It is not a question of renewing the resource of stereotypes of fear but rather of nursing the modes of their mise-en-scène. (Amossy 1991, 135–36; my translation)

In the same way, the adventure and survival horror game formula remains the same while the environment gets better and bigger. There are only seven years between *Alone in the Dark* and *SH1*, only nine between *SH1* and *SH: Homecoming*, but the improvement in the effects is stunning.

In light of the wonder expressed about the series through the years, the delight of *Silent Hill* has obviously something to do with this "aesthetic of astonishment." No different from other companies' marketing strategy, Konami has advertised *SH1* on that basis: "Stunning visuals and true-to-life CG movies coupled with horrifying 3-D images will leave you breathless" (box set). This quote has been reused with slight changes for *SH2*: "Riveting storyline, stunning graphics and true-to-life CG movies leave you on the edge of your seat" (box set). *SH3* is described in those terms: "Featuring shocking realistic graphics. . . . Series' trademark graphics possess even more disturbing detail" (box set). According to the story of its technological development, the shift from the PlayStation to the PlayStation 2 then to the PlayStation 3 has enabled the artists to improve the quality of the graphics, the atmospheric sounds, and the physics simulation. It also implies the use and creation of new tools. While *SH2* borrowed Sony's S-Force 3D Sound Library that emulates surround sound from two speakers, *SH3* uses Konami's new 5.1 sound engine.[7] If *SH2* takes advantage of the power of the emotion engine processor, a new 3-D graphics engine was created for *SH3*. Such technological progress enhances the fog and the shadow. In *SH1*, Harry is walking toward the fog, a wall never to be reached (fig. 3a). Due, as we know, to hardware limitations, this flaw is corrected in *SH2* where James is walking through a realistic volumetric fog that goes from the back to the foreground (fig. 3b). Just as the image of the silhouette of *The Exorcist*'s Father Merrin standing under a streetlamp on a foggy night in front of the possessed Reagan's house is one of the most evocative and memorable moments of contemporary horror film, the first time James is walking into the foggy Silent Hill is among the most striking events in survival horror and terror video games. This mist gets thicker from *SH3* (fig. 3c) to *SH: Homecoming*, hiding the monsters until the last minute.[8]

The water effects are few but also quite impressive in *SH2*, *SH3*, and *SH: Homecoming*, splashing and undulating in effective ways—hiding monsters so they can spring out all of a sudden. Praised from the outset, the real-time lighting is sophisticated. The flashlight of *SH1* scans the game world, revealing by its movement lurking monsters. Although it does the same thing in subsequent titles (except for *SH4: The Room*, in which Henry Townshend doesn't carry a flashlight), this light beam furthermore casts realistic and real-time shadows. The appearances of the monsters are greatly increased by their big, distorted bodies silhouetted on the floors and walls. Sometimes, as in the case of the Nurses in *SH3* and *SH: Origins,* it is their shadows that become the source of eeriness and fright, opening the door to a dual world of appearances. The dynamic flashlight dramatizes the game space. It creates its own shade and, in doing so, traces new areas of danger out of every single and simple corner of the corridor. Particularly, the flashlight animates the scene of the action. For instance, in *SH3*, the moving shadows of the subway's pillars give the disturbing impression that a monster will loom out from behind, and the silhouetted arm of a Mannequin that runs across the wall of the storeroom just might make you more distrustful (fig. 4). Carrying the fascination to the extreme, you might end up walking

Fig. 3. The fog in (a) *Silent Hill 1*, (b) *Silent Hill 2*, (c) *Silent Hill 3*

Fig. 4. *Silent Hill 3*: The silhouetted arm of a Mannequin running across the wall of the storeroom

around only to see the shadows following your move, as around Heather's school desk in *SH3*, or casting nice shadows while you follow Michelle Valdez and Lisa Garland home in *SH: Shattered Memories*.

Since the light is coming from diegetic sources, there are a few noteworthy moments in *Silent Hill*, for example, the corridor in *SH3*'s nightmarish Central Square Shopping Center with the large vent fan and the veil of black moths that Heather has to cross. The Hospital and Hell Descent levels in *SH: Homecoming* with the light coming through many vent fans are also worth mentioning. But insofar as the most virtuoso performance of the technological expertise is always the one that is the most impressive, *SH3* flaunts a real tour de force: that is, the storeroom of the nightmarish Brookhaven Hospital that comes alive (fig. 5). Instead of attempting to describe it again, I'll refer to Dan Birlew's great description:

> Inside, Heather [scanning the room with her flashlight] can see her mirror reflection. However, small lines of blood begin seeping out of the

Fig. 5. *Silent Hill 3*: Three stages of the frightening event taking place in the storeroom of the nightmarish Brookhaven Hospital

reflected sink, and soon cover the floor and walls. As you watch, blood engulfs Heather's reflection and soon her mirror image stops moving [at one point in the course of your movement]. Before she can catch a breath, lines of blood begin seeping out of the real sink standing next to her! When she tries the door, she cannot get out! The door will not open until the lines of blood have touched the door and are closing in on Heather. (2004, 115)

This scene, which occurs in real time, leaves you—to use Konami's term—breathless!

Silent Hill would not be what it is without Silent Hill. The resort town playfully points out its links to literature via its street names: for instance, you walk along (Richard) Bachman Road and (Ray) Bradbury Street in Old Silent Hill, (Dean) Koontz Street and (Michael) Crichton Street in Central Silent Hill (*SH1*), and (Jonathan) Carroll Street and (John) Saul Street in the West South Vale (*SH2* and *SH3*).[9] It is also quite amusing, on Bloch Street, to come across the word "redrum"—a reference to Stanley Kubrick's *The Shining* (1980)—written in blood on a metallic door in *SH1* (fig. 6) or the film poster of *Carrie* on the building in front of the Antique Shop.[10]

Those specific references, however, do not make the virtual Silent Hill unique. Rather, the exploration is thrilling because its meticulous design brings its virtuality precisely to the fore. Apart from the quantity of details and the quality of the textures that have increased from *SH1* to *SH: Homecoming* (and even in *SH: Shattered Memories* for the Wii—this is another story for the PS2 version), the groundwork stays the same: the buildings and their frontage are singular, some have balconies or stairs you can climb up, shop windows display their merchandise, trees and grass line the sidewalk, there are road signs, traffic lights, parked and abandoned cars, brake marks on the roadway, manholes, fire hydrants, garbage cans, public benches, phone booths, posters on the walls, bloody footprints left by the player characters when they walk in pools of blood, and so on. Each indoor location is filled with suitable props, such as the child drawings and geographical maps in classrooms, soda machines in the corridors of public places, various memos, posters, and advertisements on the walls, furniture and forms in business offices, implements and materials in construction sites, and so on.

Almost down to the smallest details,[11] the resort town is well and truly organized to welcome tourists, but one knows it is not that simple. The

Fig. 6. *Silent Hill 1*: A *clin d'oeil* (wink) at Stanley Kubrick's *The Shining* on Bloch Street

sign at the beginning of *SH2* is ample evidence: with two letters missing, it doesn't say "Welcome!" but "We com !" (fig. 7).

When Heather is exploring the Heaven's Night Club and the Brookhaven Hospital that James had previously visited, it is interesting to set foot in those places again and experience a kind of déjà vu that increases the feeling of strangeness; there is now a computer in the reception office of the hospital, and the first-aid box has been moved. The wheelchair of Alessa—associated with the one seen in the haunted house movie *The Changeling* (Peter Medak, 2000)—is discovered in weird locations. In the Hazel Street station of *SH3* leading to the Bergen Street one (as indicated on direction signs), Heather finds herself in the same subway station as Jacob at the beginning of *Jacob's Ladder*, and in similar situations, such as the twisted ride leading Jacob to the X-ray room of the hospital, which also shows familiar features. During this ride, Jacob sees at one point the crushed and mangled bicycle of his son Gabe, who had been run over, with a wheel still spinning. Then,

Fig. 7. *Silent Hill 2*: A sign at the beginning of the game

crossed corridors slowly deteriorate. The atmosphere becomes completely insane. The ceiling changes to a grate. Jacob glances at mournful patients rocking weirdly. An eerie room tone of groans and muffled screams comes from behind closed doors, while the sound of the gurney wheels seen in closed shots is heard. Blood, pieces of flesh, and limbs lie strewn on the ground. In a room, a muscular black man with no legs vibrates endlessly, his head covered with a black hood (one of the movements opening *SH3*). *Silent Hill* completely stretches out the nightmarish journey of Adrian Lyne's movie. It is not for nothing that *Jacob's Ladder* is regarded as one of the game's main inspirations. The beginning of *SH: Homecoming* and the bonus clip titled "USAGI" of *Lost Memories: The Art & Music of Silent Hill* (2003) remain direct homage to the movie's gurney ride, as is the similarity of the army jackets that both Jacob and James Sutherland (*SH2*) wear.

As for fiction emotions, a good video game character is one that you can empathize with. But when it comes to discussing artifact emotions, it should not be forgotten, as Poole points out (2000, 163), that he or she should also be aesthetically pleasing. The prerendered opening and the short clips at the beginning of *SH1*'s in-game cut-scenes give a face to the characters. Cheryl, for instance, looks angelic (much like Jacob's son), Lisa is pretty, and Dahlia has a strong, markedly superior jaw that gives her a peculiar look. The last two, as well as the police officer Cybil Bennett, have different looks in *SH: Shattered Memories*. Dahlia is younger, a rebel in her clothing, and shows an unexpected sexual drive (during the car drive with Harry, it is quite a surprise when she talks about "Sid and Nancy," i.e., her "tits"). Again, the technological progress has been an asset as well. The transitions to prerendered CG movies are really smooth in *SH2*. *SH3* and its followers have all the in-game cut-scenes that enable great characterization. Heather is not Lara Croft, but the character designers (Shingo Yuri, Minako Asano, and Sachiko Sugawara) based her on Sophie Marceau and Charlotte Gainsbourg. They gave her some sex appeal in a fairly discreet way (Beuglet 2003). One has to view the makings of *SH2* and *SH3* to realize that the designers paid great attention to the NPCs and tried to give them and the protagonists as much emotional expression as possible. *SH2*'s character designer and CGI creator Takayoshi Sato explains how the main heroine Maria, whose face has the same polygon structure as Mary's, possesses much more appeal and looks more real than scientist Aki Ross of *Final Fantasy: The Spirits Within* (Hironobu Sakaguchi and Moto Sakakibara, 2001). For him, there is a reason: she is not perfect, she has wrinkles, and (the narrator of Beuglet 2003 adds) flaunts her tummy with a little roll of flab and does not try to conceal the brown spots on her skin. Sato has also designed the characters of Angela and Eddie in order to reveal specific aspects of their personalities. He makes Angela look older with a facial emotion that seems a little bit uncomfortable, and gives Eddie wider pupils, his eyes looking in two directions, one moving a little fast compared to the other. In *SH3,* Yuri, Asano, and Sugawara give Claudia no eyebrows, managing to provoke subtle and uneasy feelings without revealing her malevolent side too obviously. They dress Vincent in nice clothes and give him a neat appearance, but make him laugh as if he is hiding something nasty. Since his eyes are squinted, one of his eyes does not look at the observer while he speaks. Detective Cartland, inspired by the priest in *The Fifth Element* (Luc Besson, 1997), is old and losing his hair. Yuri confesses that he's going bald and doesn't want anyone to notice; that's why he combs his hair back so that nobody will see his bald spot.

The monsters are not to be outdone. Masahiro Ito explains that his hideous and grotesque visions come from the works of painters such as Francis Bacon (*SH2*) and Hieronymus Bosch (*SH3*), among others. Sato adds elsewhere the names of Andrew Wyeth and Rembrandt to the visual influences on *SH2* (Perry 2001b). It is also difficult not to think about Hans Bellmer's dolls. With their scenes lit by a halo of light, their use of chiaroscuro, and their figures emerging from the dark, Caravaggio and Georges de La Tour are, among others, probably part of *Silent Hill*'s artistic background too.

A Cinematic Experience

Movies have been mentioned a great deal so far, and not without reason. If there is one expression from Konami's own advertising that has been repeated throughout all of the games, it's probably the notion that *Silent Hill* delivers a "cinematic horror experience" (box set of *SH1* and *SH2*). In "Discursively Constructing the Art of Silent Hill" (2010), Ewan Kirkland also shows how the series is defined as art and is linked to art cinema in the *Making of SH2*. The two DVDs distributed by Konami as extra or promotional materials, *The Art of Silent Hill* (2001) and *Lost Memories: The Art & Music of Silent Hill* (2003)—released for the PlayStation Portable as *The Silent Hill Experience* (2006)—could be added here too.

Most certainly, the cut-scenes, or cinematics as it would be relevant to call them here, take on the language of film. If they create fiction emotions, it is also because they benefit from what cinema already knows. It is difficult not to be aware of their formal characteristics, particularly for someone like me coming from film studies. The cut-scenes' shots are directed and cut together in a way that makes their viewing compelling. It's a camera movement pulling away from Harry that, interestingly, reveals the presence of Cybil in the Cafe 5to2 at the beginning of *SH1*. The camera moves slowly during their talk to get away from simple talking heads and to compose a more dynamic scene. Dahlia Gillespie makes her appearance in the Balkan Church through a CG movie's crane shot down on a crucifix and away from her. While she talks about the Flauros, a low-angle shot shows her under the crucifix. When Harry goes to the waterworks, the scene ends with Lisa isolated in a shot that expresses her loneliness. Her death is intensified by the sad music (a guitar theme quite different from the synthesized themes of other cut-scenes) and by the camera moving toward Harry as the dying

Lisa is heard knocking behind the closed door. In *SH2,* the camera is just as mobile during the first and second encounters between James and Angela. In many cut-scenes, it often moves rather subtly. Other movements, like the crane shot before James jumps into the third abyss of the Toluca Prison, are also quite impressive. Maria's deaths are deeply touching because of how they are made. At the time of Maria's first death, after he runs away from Pyramid Head, James's panic in front of the closed elevator doors is sharpened by the shaky camera and the closed framing over his shoulder. When an ear-splitting noise shifts to a tearful piano melody after Maria has been stabbed and killed behind the doors, it is hard to struggle against the sadness. The gamer aware that the scene is a construction will be touched by the making of it. This strange kind of sadness, as Marcia Eaton would say, is even more intense when James suddenly realized his murderous gesture in Room 312 of the Lake View Hotel. It is framed in a long shot in front of the television, and the camera slowly turns around behind him on a variation of the main piano theme until Laura gets in. Then, leaving time and space for the emotion, a long shot shows the two far away after James has made his confession. From this time on, closer to a *Final Fantasy: The Spirits Within* than a *Toy Story,* the cut-scenes of *SH3* are true cinematic pieces. They now perfectly play with the lens's focus, as demonstrated by the first time Heather has a throbbing headache after her first talk with Claudia. A limited depth of field, an optical phenomenon common to all cinema camera lenses, is used in the dramatic moment at the Lakeside Amusement Park, where Heather walks away while Douglas is seen out of focus behind her pointing his gun at her back.

To assume that the relationship between *Silent Hill* and cinema is limited solely to the cut-scenes would result in the pure and simple refutation of the definition of video games—not movies—as a cinematic experience. Evidently, this asks for further considerations. At the image level, the likeness to film is marked in *SH2* with the noise effect, a grainy filter that gives the illusion it was shot on film stock. An extra setting option that has enthused Imamura: "We're really proud of the analog film kind of style. We wanted to create a non-polygonal-looking image, and that's why the game has the noisy look" (Davison 2001, 126). The additional layer is renewed in *SH3* and "used [again] to create a scarier atmosphere" (instruction manual). This time, "The development team wished to give *Silent Hill 3* a distorted look, closer to watching an old horror movie on VHS tape" (Birlew 2004, 35). *SH: Origins* adds dirt and scratches on the already grainy celluloid image during

Fig. 8. *Silent Hill 1*: A lens flare

fights with monsters; they are also added in *SH4: The Room* when ghosts appear—during short dying cut-scenes and during the passages through the hole connecting the different worlds. But even with a lower-resolution image, *SH1* has a filmlike appearance. Michael Riser reminds us of this in his review of *SH3*: "The original *Silent Hill* still looks quite attractive for a PS title, but there's something far more important about it: it gave the series' art style its roots" (2003). Consequently, a more obvious visible (and to become very popular) element gives the series its visual style: the lens flare effect simulating the glow-over part of the image caused by a source of light hitting the lens of a camera. While there is no sun in Silent Hill (as compared to Liberty and Vice cities of the *Grand Theft Auto* series) to create such an aesthetic impression, each time you stare into the lens with your flashlight, it creates such flares (fig. 8).

The use of cinematic camera angles and different camera positions is not a new stylistic trait unique to *Silent Hill*. Such a vertical angle is used to show Edward in a corridor of Derceto in *Alone in the Dark*, and also at the beginning of *Resident Evil 2*, showing Leon running in the back street behind the gun shop. A similar shot in *SH1* follows Harry in the alley where Cheryl has entered. However, the directors of the first three games of the series (*SH1*'s Keiichiro Toyama, *SH2*'s Masahi Tsuboyama, and *SH3*'s Kazuhide Nakazawa) have done a really great job making the montage of their action more expressive and dynamic. They do not divert the attention away from information. On the contrary, the camera cuts to a new shot in order to point out the entrance of the next location or to draw attention to the presence of items. The player characters are always turning their heads to look at those important elements. If Gordon's house is not marked on the map, there is a notable cut to the alley that indicates to Harry the back access to this teacher's house. Of course, as in any survival horror game, Tsuboyama and his fellows play with the field of action in order to hide monsters off-screen once in a while. The Nurse's sudden appearance when James enters Room M3 of the Brookhaven Hospital is a good example of these scary moments. Indoors, where montage is most often displayed, the directors keep the over-the-shoulder/head view when you get back in a corridor to set off the player character's movement. But their preset camera positions and angles upon the entrance to a room vary superbly. They reposition the camera from the back to the front of the room, from a low to a high angle, from lighting the enemies frontally or leaving them in back light, and so on. With the power of *SH3*'s graphics engine, Nakazawa is able to compose exceptional frames leaving us in awe, as in the low-angle shot through the wheel of a wheelchair, spinning when Heather moves forward in the basement of the Brookhaven Hospital, or the breathtaking image in the room of the church that Heather explores to find the cassette tape (fig. 9).

One is still astonished at how beautiful this may be upon viewing James in *SH2* through the big ceiling fan in the room where he gets the Great Knife of Pyramid Head, or seeing a Flying Reptile moving around Harry in *SH2* and passing just in front the airborne camera in the rear foreground. The vertical angle in the women's restroom of *SH: Origins*' Cedar Groove Sanitarium with the blood inscription "Bring me my son" is quite impressive as well.

The movements of the virtual camera are what sets *SH1* apart from the first *Alone in the Dark* and *Resident Evil* games. Along with the vertical angle, the camera follows Harry in the alley at the beginning of the game. Actually, from the moment Harry crosses the fence and arrives in the alley, only two high-angle shots are fixed. Otherwise, the camera does not stop moving. It

Fig. 9. *Silent Hill 3*: Two beautiful shots showing Heather Mason, first in the basement of the Brookhaven Hospital, then in a room of the church

Fig. 10. *Silent Hill 1*: The camera moving to frame Harry Mason through pipes

moves in a peculiar manner to show the distressed father through several pipes (fig. 10), rises up, and looks down vertically as he reaches a corner.

Then the camera drops low to follow his footpath. There is a similar shot when Harry comes across a wheelchair after the night has strangely fallen. But this time, the virtual camera stays in the air, following and making circular movements with Harry as he bumps into a gurney with a bloody corpse under a white sheet. While the player character moves on, the camera suddenly gets closer, as if something was about to happen (a move often repeated at the beginning of *SH2* too). Yet nothing happens until Harry is attacked by little monsters at the end of the alley, starts to flee, and realizes that he seems to be trapped. The camera then moves and whirls round as restlessly as Harry himself does. This dynamic beginning is representative of the moving camera aesthetic of *Silent Hill.* It is not only during the cutscenes that the camera is almost constantly moving. It follows the player character in action from the front, the side, or behind. What's more, with the exception of a few locations (the alley being one example), the camera can be controlled with a "search view" (L2 button in *SH1* to *SH: Origins*), which fixes the camera at a certain distance behind the player character (like the camera in *Tomb Raider*, which swirls around a lot too, but not with the same effect). So even if you cannot switch to a subjective point of view, as it is possible to do with the camera obscura in the *Fatal Frame* series (there is a first-person point of view in *SH: Homecoming*; however, it is only useful for looking around, as it is not possible to make the player character move once you have engaged the R3 button), this over-the-shoulder view allows you to see what's coming up around the next turn. Nevertheless, the search view does not always toe the line.[12] As has often been underlined regarding the survival horror genre, the controls remain unwieldy, introducing chilling—or, for some gamers, frustrating—moments. For example, while James explores porches on Lindsey Street, whether holding the L2 button or not, the camera remains behind trees, blocking the view. This makes you worried about what could happen out of your sight. Consequently, standing too close to a monster keeps you from framing it effectively, making closed fights difficult. And even more significantly, every time you hit the L2 button, the camera quickly twirls around to get into position behind the player character, a movement that may make you feel dizzy and bewildered.

Although reviewers were not specific, it is on this basis that a comparison with *The Shining* becomes relevant, and Cynthia Freeland's comments about Kubrick's film are enlightening. Freeland observes:

> The camera in *The Shining* is a particularly eerie and disorienting force. One reviewer [Steven Shiff of the *Boston Phoenix*] commented, "Most of the film feels like an endless subjective shot: we appear to be watching the hotel and its occupants through the eyes of an unearthly prowler, someone who sees very differently from the way we see." Even the more straightforward passages that represent dialogue or lay out the hotel's rooms and corridors become uncanny through unusual camera motions or perspectives. (Freeland 2000, 217)

With the moving camera during the dialogue cut-scenes and the outdoor explorations representing long takes, *Silent Hill* gives the same impression. At first glance, since you are controlling the player character and the third-person point of view as well, one could easily think you remain this unearthly prowler. As for the camera's dislocation from its normal vantage point in many scenes of Kubrick's film, the fact that you cannot continuously and completely command the roving virtual camera provides it with some supernatural powers. "It almost acts as if it has a will of its own, conjuring up the independent evil forces that reside in the Overlook Hotel [for *The Shining* and in the entire town for *Silent Hill*]" (Freeland 2000, 219). To watch the scene from a distance also conveys "the feeling that [you] cannot see exactly what is going on and must creep forward to find out" (218). Insofar as you are to discover disturbing sights, the progress is always punishing. That's what Danny is experiencing in the Overlook Hotel.

> Mounted just below [above in actual fact] the level of a Big Wheels tricycle, the camera tracks Jack's son Danny (Danny Lloyd) as he races around corners and down the hotel's long corridors. We come close to occupying Danny's point of view in terms of both position and motion, but our perspective is not quite identified with his in these scenes. Instead, we follow behind him like a force that keeps him in view for unknown, perhaps nefarious, ends. (Freeland 2000, 218)

Seeing the games in the light of cinema, one can only point out the similarity between the muted swaying of the Steadicam tracking shots preceding or following Danny, Jack (Jack Nicholson), or his wife Wendy (Shelley Duvall) in *The Shining*'s corridors of the hotel and the camera movements physically linked to *Silent Hill*'s player characters' movements in the various indoor locations.

Extending the parallel further to include even earlier occurrences, the roving camera in *Silent Hill* may even be related to the "unchained camera" of the German expressionism, a device that aimed to articulate the character's inner feelings. In fact, the mental state of the protagonists, the role played by the town, the blur effect of the fog, the lighting style, the high- or low-angle shots, all the prominent visual features of *Silent Hill* enable a comparison with this school's aesthetic (an aesthetic borrowed later by the American film noir of the 1940s and 1950s). As a key movement in the development of the horror film, the German movement displays a "haunted screen," and "what matters is to create states of anxiety and terror" (Eisner 1973, 21). From the pictorial and theatrical *Cabinet of Dr. Caligari* (Robert Weine, 1919) to expressionist films such as *Nosferatu, a Symphony of Horror* (Friedrich W. Murnau, 1922) and *The Golem* (Paul Wegner, 1920), and even to a *Kammerspiel* (chamber drama) like *The Last Laugh* (Murnau, 1924), which makes particular use of an "unchained camera," the German movement's principal objective is the portrayal of psychological states through external forms, those of the world's spaces and the objects within them. To carry off this effect, the image is distorted by various means such as diagonal compositions, depth of field integrating characters in settings and landscapes (which become "dramatic" or "dramaturgic" factors), camera angles, light and shadows. To refer to the last aspect, as with *Silent Hill*'s use of the flashlight for the main source of illumination, the expressionists' lighting shapes the space of the drama, generates a new area of high contrast and black shadows, traces the contour and the contours of things, casts a world of shadows, and creates effects of chiaroscuro. This renders architecture expressive, dissolves bodies in dusk or obscurity, and gives a symbolic dimension to the pictorial representation. The main goal of the expressionist movement is to depict a *stimmung*, that is, to suggest the "vibrations of the soul." In the context of German film, this "mood," "atmosphere," or "attunement" of the image "hovers around objects as well as people: it is a 'metaphysical' accord, a mystical and singular harmony amid the chaos of things, a kind of sorrowful nostalgia which . . . is mixed with well-being, an imprecise nuance of nostalgia, languor colored with desire, lust of body and soul" (Eisner 1973, 199). Dennis Giles in "The Conditions of Pleasure in Horror Cinema" comments,

> The *stimmung* . . . is bent by fear, desire and anticipation so that it "speaks" something more than it shows. The figure of the delayed, partial or empty vision ambiguates the image; it overlays the explicit significance of the scene with a monstrous presence which belongs to an *other* scene—a scene off-screen, and not fully conscious. (1984, 42)

In one of the figural categories Giles distinguishes, the on-scene threat represented by the presence of the monster is obscured by the shadows of a chiaroscuro lighting pattern as well as by the mist, an element highly relevant with regard to *Silent Hill*. Giles talks about the masking "spectral light" of *Poltergeist* (Tobe Hooper, 1982) and the way the light glares into the camera. The artifact emotions thus come to the surface from images that can "evoke an ambiguous *stimmung* of combined threat and wonder" (Giles 1984, 43). And then, in an afterword, Giles makes a point of noting that sound "works to reinforce or intensify the threat of the visual figure" and "communicates an other scene while yet withholding it from full presence" (48). This way of bending the *stimmung* is most certainly one of the distinctive, stylistic features of *Silent Hill*.

Audio-Video Games

To begin a short essay on the importance of sound in the video game, Jonathan Hoffberg (1997) recalls an earlier MIT study in which participants had to choose the best-looking picture between a high-definition television with a low-fidelity sound system and the same content shown on a regular television outfitted with a CD-quality sound system. The participants chose the normal NTSC screen with the high-fidelity sound. If sound generally makes a picture look better, it can also be said that it makes a terrifying one even more frightening by its force of suggestion, by getting deeper in the unconscious. From this auditory perspective, *Silent Hill* is undoubtedly without equal within the genre. Here it is relevant to quote a comment from French sound theoretician Michel Chion about David Lynch's work in a section on *Eraserhead*:

> Lynch can be said to have renewed the cinema by way of sound. If his visual continuity is classic and transparent (though with a kind of warp which once again reveals the force of cinema, as a slight change in the conventional rules yields a wealth of new effects), his sound continuity is idiosyncratic from the outset. Sound has a precise function, propelling us through the film, giving us the sense of being inside it, wrapped within its timespan. The sound is animated from the inside by a perpetual pulsation. (Chion 1995, 44)

To start with, if the pulsation places you in a secure inner space in *Eraserhead* according to Chion, it is quite the opposite in *Silent Hill*. Be that as it may, it can also be said that *Silent Hill* (re)vamps the survival horror genre from the beginning by the way the game uses sound. Sound director (for *SH1*, *SH2*, *SH3*, and *SH4: The Room*) and series music composer Akira Yamaoka has left his mark on the genre.

To bring into play the title of another Chion book, *Audio-Vision: Sound on Screen* (1994), the games of *Silent Hill* are really "audio-video" games, and, it is important to note, the audio precedes the video in the expression. This is the primary point of Guillaume Roux-Girard's essay, "Listening to Fear: A Study of Sound in Horror Computer Games" (2010): sound is at the core of the scary experience of the survival horror genre. As *SH1* was a team creation from the beginning, the game, and incidentally the series, was designed with sound in mind (which is not always the case in video games). With the key visual device of the series—the flashlight with its limited halo and range of illumination—comes an important audio device: the pocket radio; it transmits only white noise when there are enemies nearby (both devices are absent in *SH4: The Room*). Along with the fog and the darkness, this audiovisual combination works very well to fulfill a precept of sound design put forward by Randy Thom in "Designing a Movie for Sound": "Starving the eye will inevitably bring the ear, and therefore the imagination, more into play" (1999). As I also state in "Sign of a Threat: The Effects of Warning Systems in Survival Horror Games," the impact of this forewarning in eliciting fear is enormous (but here I'm referring to a type of emotion elicited by the gameplay, a type I'll be talking in the next chapter). When the presence of an enemy is signified through static, you are suddenly more afraid of the dark, taking each step forward with more watchful eye and ear. The first sounds you hear in *SH1* of the approaching of a monster through the radio are among the most striking events in survival horror and terror. Moreover, when made aware of this presence, either on the left or behind you, you become much more conscious of the use of (surround) sound—emulated in *SH2* and effective in *SH3* and latter games.

You are also kept on your toes in *Silent Hill,* and more specifically in *SH1,* by haunting horror noises without visible or identifiable sources that randomly startle you, or that help build the fearsome atmosphere, like hearing a sobbing child in the Men's Rest Room on the second floor of the Midwich Elementary School, and the plaintive cry in the sewers leading to the amusement park (*SH1*), or the single, short baby's cry near Room 203 of the Wood Side Apartments, and the little, high-pitched groaning beast in the basement of Brookhaven Hospital (*SH2*). While the cat hiding in one of the boxes of the school's locker room makes you jump when it springs out, it is equally scary to hear a monster bolt when the cat escapes out of the room (*SH1*). You hear the neighbors' story from above in the storage room of the Central Square Shopping Center of *SH3* and in the restroom of the fifth floor of the construction site before the Hilltop Center. Sometimes things suddenly burst out when you are leaving rooms in both hospitals (in a restroom, the storeroom, the director's office after you take the Plate of Queen for *SH1,* or Room C2 for *SH2*). Harmless Little Phantoms in *SH1,* which are almost transparent and can easily get near you, produce a screeching sound that sets your teeth on edge. The creatures of *SH: Shattered Memories* also have a high-pitched scream. In *SH2,* a never-to-be-seen roaring monster follows James along the hiking path at the beginning, and small, unseen beasts rustle in the leaves as well.

To demonstrate the use of sound in storytelling, Randy Thom gives an example of particular relevance to the narratives in *Silent Hill*. He talks about a man returning to his hometown in an attempt to find the source of his bad dreams. More specifically, the man goes back to the steel mill where his father worked.

> First, it will be natural to tell the story more-or-less through the pov [point of view] of our central character. But that's not all. A steel mill gives us a huge palette for sound. Most importantly, it is a place which we can manipulate to produce a set of sounds which range from banal to exciting to frightening to weird to comforting to ugly to beautiful. The place can therefore become a character, and have its own voice, with a range of "emotions" and "moods." And the sounds of the mill can resonate with a wide variety of elements elsewhere in the story. None of this good stuff is likely to happen unless we write, shoot, and edit the story in a way that allows it to happen. (Thom 1999)

Team Silent allows itself all the possibilities. There is no steel mill in Silent Hill, but there may as well be. Thus, if the prominent string orchestration of *Resident Evil* and its sound effects brings it closer to the classic use of sound in horror films, Akira Yamaoka seems to be, and I'm borrowing the expression from a review of *SH1 Original Soundtrack* (1999),[13] conducting in a giant factory that manufactures evil. Because Yamaoka's musical themes, often compared to Angelo Badalamenti's *Twin Peaks* pieces, are mostly kept for the cut-scenes. The themes range from simple synthesized musical scores in *SH1* to the more trip-hop songs of *SH3*, of which the song "Letter—From the Lost Days" that accompanies the long cut-scene in the car journey to Silent Hill gives a very emotional scope to Heather's account of her past. Consequently, Yamaoka has composed marvelously dark ambient and industrial soundscapes for the gameplay. In his "orchestra," the strings, percussion, and wind instruments also have their dark counterparts, which means they give up their places to all kinds of industrial and metal noises: bang, clang, drone, grinding, hammer, rattle, scrape, screech, slam, throb, and so on. Heavy tracks such as "Until Death," "Devil's Cry," and "Half Day" or more quiet ones such as "Hear Nothing" and "Killed by Death" of the *SH1 Original Soundtrack* give a really good indication of the range of

Yamaoka's work. The more you progress in Silent Hill, the deeper you go in its nightmarish depths, the more the sounds relentlessly hum and pound. If they rush you to act in many places, every so often the repetitive industrial beats eventually become almost unbearable and alienating, raising terror to another level. As Carr says, "*Silent Hill* wants its players to be frightened, and the sounds of the gameworld move into our own space" (2006, 60). The sounds go even further because Yamaoka takes a different approach than do other survival horror sound designers. As he explains:

> I think that the sounds in *Resident Evil* are pretty formal. I would say we are used to hearing them. Whereas for *Silent Hill 2,* I really tried to create something that would surprise you, something that would challenge your imagination as if the sounds were going under your skin. What I mean by that is to create a physical reaction for the game player such as a feeling of apprehension and unease. (Beuglet 2001)

In addition to the industrial orchestration, the roars and shrieks of all sorts of monsters are also disturbing for their peculiarities, while the Doctors of *SH1* walk around groaning like zombies. As for their bodily nature, the sound expressions of the monsters evolve. The Nurses become sexier through the series and leave their low-pitched "voice" of *SH1* and penetrating, sped-up respiration in *SH3* for much more noiseless behaviors in *SH: Origins* and *SH: Homecoming.* The Little Monsters at Midwich Elementary School have mournful cries and insane screams when they jump on Harry. The numerous Patient Demons of *SH2* walk with an unsteady gait and sound like rusting, rolling mechanical toys when they are on the floor. As Yamaoka explains in the *Making of SH3,* he mixes digital effects with real animal noises, a mix that puts you off balance between recognition, uncertainty, and fear. For example, the Double Heads Dogs roar like lions, the Closers breathe and charge like rhinoceroses, and the Numb Bodies bray like donkeys and screech like monkeys before they die.

Although the ear-splitting industrial noises are important features of Silent Hill sound design, Yamaoka does not resort solely on them. He uses a huge palette of sounds. The moment Harry sets foot in Silent Hill, you can hear the "evil steel mill" in the distance. A hollow rumbling drone arouses the feeling that the ghost town is groaning, answering to important events with its notorious siren (although I have no recollection of hearing it in *SH3* though). In *SH2,* the addition of faint water drippings during the day adds a tenebrous dimension to the atmosphere. The eerie atmospheric rumbling is only broken by your footsteps on the foggy roadway, the static of the pocket radio, the encounters with the monsters, and the blasts of the handgun or the blows of the wood plank. This rumbling changes through the games, from a drone to a screech on the way to the Antique Shop (*SH1*) for example, or with the addition of squirming and swarming sounds at night in *SH2*. But perhaps more distressing, indoor locations, or many parts of them, are totally noiseless. In the sewers and the Hazel Street Subway Station, the pocket radio does not function; you can only hear the sounds of your footsteps[14] and of the locked/opened doors breaking into the dark. "The job of a sound designer," says Yamaoka, "is not just to create sounds, so to speak. We also have to know how to use silence. I think that selecting moments of silence is another way of producing sound" (Beuglet 2001). Obviously, what would Silent Hill be without its dead silence? Its uncomfortable quietness makes you feel the solitude of the night, makes you become aware, in a combination of threat and wonder as it was described earlier, of the solitary experience of the game. This feeling is colored by other room tones. For instance, the normal Alchemilla Hospital of *SH1* gives you the impression that you are undersea in a submarine, an effect the sewers intensify with the water dripping and the muffled echo of footsteps on metal grates. But if the confrontation with the monsters rambling in the corridors reminds you that you still have to survive the resort town, the dark and industrial ambiences also make it clear that you have to carry on with your journey, that there is an evil intelligence that exhorts you to do so. The continuation of Chion's early talk about Lynch offers another great insight:

> Given its fundamentally temporal nature, sound (far more than the image) is ordinarily likened to a continuum, a flow, and used in this way. However, in Lynch's work, the pulsation of sound environments does not give rise to a flow which overrides the cuts. The pulsation is perpetually stopped and started by scissors which at once separate and join, often in synch with the visual cuts. The author controls the pulsation like a flow, which he interrupts to distribute and regulate it in spurts. (1995, 44)

Once more, this comment about the sound environments applies to *Silent Hill*. As there are breathing tempos with voodoo incantations in some rare moments, the heartbeat of Silent Hill, and by the way of the gamer, is greatly variable. At any time pounding sounds may break out, alarming sounds may fade in and out, and an ambience may overlap across different spaces. However, the pulsation separating and joining the visual "cuts" is also salient. The end of cut-scenes recurrently brings about the end of the musical theme or a change in ambience. Contrary to the music of *Resident Evil*, which is used for sound bridges over the doorways to the rooms, the short black transitions through the doors of *Silent Hill* draw more upon the notion of a "cut." At first, the pocket radio's static constantly breaks the silence and punctuates the comings and goings in the different rooms. On the one hand, as in the Wood Side Apartments of *SH2*, it is the corridors that are filled with silence and the rooms that are inhabited by dark or odd ambiences. On the other hand, most often in the nightmarish world, it is the opposite; the corridors are searched on industrial noises, while the entrance to the rooms leads to more quiet audio spaces. If rooms are normally filled with monsters lying in wait for you, a few others are empty of their presence, but not of the noises. This is especially the case in the room with the huge fan near the storage in the nightmarish Midwich Elementary School, the one in Nowhere in which the sound of lightbulbs bursting is heard (*SH1*), and the other in the nightmarish Hilltop Center with the Slurper in a cage (*SH3*). Since you cannot hear the ambience of a room through the door, and the radio does not pick up their presence through them either, the sounds often arrive in bursts.

Playful Design

The audiovisual qualities of *Silent Hill* have earned it much praise, as this eulogistic statement by Lorenzo Bassanelli demonstrates: "*Silent Hill 2* is a fascinating, beautiful game. Through a series of courageous stylistic choices, the developers have created a game that is pure art" (2001). Many emotions based on the artifact are elicited along the journey. There is no doubt that the cinematographic comparison is in great part responsible for such enthusiasm. However, it is necessary to tell the seventh (cinema) and the tenth (video game) arts apart.

As Ewan Kirkland argues pertinently, *Silent Hill* "constitutes an extremely self-reflexive series, frequently acknowledging its videogame status and interrogating the medium as experience and text" (2007, 403), whose "aspects heighten rather than undermine the games' horror effect. The games encourage critical reflection upon aspects of videogaming, while maintaining a visceral hold on the player" (414). From the moment the terrifying dream starts, *SH: Homecoming* is seen as a recurrence of the other beginnings of the series. The pink bunny links *SH: Homecoming*'s nightmare to the one in *SH3* and *SH4: The Room*. The final revelation about Alex's journey to save his young brother seems to replay or copy James's to meet Mary. When you are aware of these parallels, *Silent Hill* is seen as a series, as a videoludic artifact. Is it necessary to say that, as a "re-imagining of the original Silent Hill that turns everything you thought you knew on its head" (Konami website),[15] *SH: Shattered Memories* remains a true self-reflexive game (not like the play novel adaptation of *SH1* on the Game Boy Advance in 2001)? You meet characters you got to know before and go to places you have already been, yet everything is changed from your memories. While the end credits are rolling, there is another self-reflexive twist in the story. Dr. Kaufman's Initial Assessment, which is typed, is not about Cheryl, but about the gamer. The final statement says: "Patient in a word: a 'do-er'. So ... summing up. Am sure patient will be back—lots of uncovered ground. Don't believe we've seen everything yet. Might be worth going back to the start and re-examining with benefit of what we know now. Think patient will agree!" This other statement is aimed at the replay value of *SH: Shattered Memories*: "The game watches you and adapts to your actions to create a unique experience to each player and intensify their fears" (Konami website). If your actions and answers to Dr. Kaufman's little therapy games change the way the characters appear, so will the locations the player character can access and the scenes you'll see. This design is also reminiscent of the ultimate goal of interactive fiction, which wanted to make the reader a writer of the story. Dr. Kaufman's sessions are referring me to the one conducted by Dr. Turner at the exit polls of each chapter of the interactive movie *Tender Loving Care* (Rob Landeros and David Wheeler, 1999). There too, the action is changed according to the ways you answer the questions, revolving in great part about sex (see Perron 2003).

The artifact emotions felt during a game are not only based on the awareness of its plot construction or the tours de force of its audio-vision, they also come from the consciousness of the operation of that intelligence behind the game design. The experience of *SH: Shattered Memories* can be pleasurable because it focuses "on escape and evasion rather than direct confrontation" (Konami website) as it is found in the classical formula of survival horror genre. In the same way, you can be delighted by the way the Wiimote enables you to move the flashlight. Another example of striking game design can be seen at the beginning of *SH2*, when James comes across a well and it turns out to be a save point. Knowing the convention of the survival horror genre where save points precede a new area or a difficult fight, you move on with some hesitation. However, you only end up encountering the harmless Angela in a cut-scene located in the graveyard. The apprehension is therefore developed through the gamer's horizon of expectations. It is the game that is thus seen as the artifact. Another assertion about *SH2* from a review raises a significant issue:

> It is possible that a game such as *Silent Hill 2* puts forward another hypothesis, that of a *mutation*: rather than come to a standstill, cinema has been going on to find other spectators. . . . That a game rests, at this point, on its atmosphere, in other words on its aesthetic force, leaves no surprise, no obligation of result, performance, but a real experience of spectator, who will also be a bit director, free to go where he wants, see what he wants. *SH* is a slow game, frightening but also very beautiful, which makes of time a space where move our anguishes, a strange condensable or stretchable ribbon on demand. (Bénédict 2002, 58; my translation)

Insofar as *Silent Hill* communicates in a great manner through eyes and ears, it is a real audio-viewing experience. However that may be, the series remains a gaming experience. In that sense, it is indeed seeking out another type of spectator, mostly through the creation of a new type of emotions.

CHAPTER 4

Gamers' Terrifying Exploration of *Silent Hill*

> In a video game, the emotional engine that guarantees that the player remains there, playing the game, is the gameplay, which is already a scenario in itself: it puts forth a specific objective, gives you a means to reach it, and then places obstacles in your way.
>
> —David Neiss, Rayman 3's *scenario writer*

Gameplay Emotions

The analysis of fiction emotions and artifact emotions remains relevant to the study of *Silent Hill*. The resort town and the stories that take place there are complex and compelling. They are part of the game. Needless to say, any study of the series cannot be reduced to an account of these sole aspects. Although story-driven games such as *Silent Hill* rest on the fate of characters, playing them is not about viewing a movie (there is Christophe Gans's film adaptation for such experience). As Susana Pajares Tosca notes in a reading of *Resident Evil: Code Veronica X* (Capcom / Capcom 2001) that can also be applied here:

> Once the game starts, we work at two levels: that of the plot, where [Wolfgang] Iser's gaps are applicable, and that of the game, where the problems we encounter have to be solved, not interpreted. Our mind is busy with the plot level and the action level at the same time. The first

one, that we experience on the fly, can be narrated afterwards (it is *tellable*) and makes sense as a story (complete with character motivation and feelings); the second is about solving action problems, and if it was to be narrated it would correspond to what we know as walkthroughs. (2003, 211)

Playing a game goes beyond simple narrative comprehension or wonder at its cinematic way of depicting the action. One must grasp the video game's contemporary specificity. As I like to point out,[1] the famous and widely influential French journal *Cahiers du cinéma* (cradle of the French New Wave, the notion of mise-en-scène, and the "politique des auteurs") has so wisely remarked upon both the medium's evolution and its merit:

> Henceforth, the video game no longer needs to imitate the cinema to exist because it proposes hypotheses that cinema has never been able to formulate, as well as emotions of another nature. If video games have looked to the cinema in the past (their designers are also moviegoers), today they allow us to look at the cinema differently, to question it in its modes of functioning and its theoretical principles. Video games are not only a social phenomenon, they are the essential crossroads of a redefinition of our relation to the narrative world in images, prolonging what Godard formulated ("A film: between the active and the passive, between the actor and the spectator") without knowing that the video game was going to seize this question, to reply to this demand, while leaving the cinema without reply. (Higuinen and Tesson 2002a, 5; my translation)

If film has been understood for some time now as working on our senses of sight and hearing in order to produce a much more visceral experience than any other art (see, for instance, Plantinga 1995), the video game has certainly invaded this hallowed ground. Again, in a comparison with horror cinema, survival horror is the perfect videoludic genre to expound the creation by the tenth art, of "emotions of another nature." I call these *gameplay emotions*, emotions that arise from our actions in the game—mostly in the game world in the case of narrative games—and the consequent reactions of the game and game world.

In studying films, Tan stresses that the action tendency—the inclination to initiate, maintain, or alter a relationship with the environment (1996, 45)[2] and the urge to act in one way or another until an emotional episode is closed due to a change of situation—is not actual fact, but only virtual.

> There is nothing one can do except watch or turn away. In the case of film viewing [as compared to watching a football game in a stadium] the choices are even more limited. All we can see is what is on the screen; our gazes are directed automatically to the spot where the action is.
>
> Thus, in effect, the action repertoire of the viewer in his or her capacity of spectator to the fictional events is empty. (Tan 1996, 75)

As noted in the second chapter regarding the plot level, the emotional experience of spectators is based on their lack of control. They have no choice but to assume an observational attitude. Tan comes up with a "slightly grisly metaphor"[3] to define the status of the spectator in the diegesis: "the subject in fiction is actually a head without a body, which is placed on a cart by an obliging assistant [the 'editorial intelligence' behind the narration that can manipulate the viewer] and wheeled—or even flown—around through the time and space of the fictional world" (1996, 241). The spectator's inability to take action maximizes the creation of fiction emotions because of the guarantee of a safe involvement. However, it is also minimized because of the enslavement to the "obliging assistant" who sets before you each and every event the assistant wishes you to see.

In studying video games, it is easy to recognize the difference between the positing of the spectator and the positing of the gamer. The latter is able to participate in the display of the game world, to act within the town of Silent Hill through Travis, Harry, Heather, James, Henry, or Alex. In accordance with Steven Poole's subtle wording, "In the cinema, the world is projected *at* you, in a videogame, you are projected *into* the world" (2000, 98). Therefore, to refer to Tan's "grisly" metaphor, the gamer is a subject who has gotten back, not his/her own body, but a specular body in third-person perspective of the survival horror. As his/her ergodic activity is fundamental to, say, walking through Silent Hill, he/she has in return "corporealized pleasures in video games."[4] That is the *mutation* of cinema, of the other spectator the concluding quotation in the previous chapter is talking about. In concrete terms, the gamer has recovered the use of his hands through the DualShock Analog Controller, and of his arms and upper body through the Wii remote and the nunchuk, with the help of which he moves through and around the time and space of the fictional world. Compared to the spectator, he well and truly possesses, via the controls, a repertoire of actions. We should not forget the conclusion by Petri Lankoski, which is based on an analysis of *SH3*, that a player character is not only characterized by his predefined functions such as his look, gestures, or predesigned dialogue, but also by his goals and subgoals in the game, and by the actions he can and cannot perform (Lankoski 2005). In *Silent Hill*, for example, he may walk, run, sidestep right or left, turn 180 degrees, search, look in, turn a flashlight on and off, draw a weapon in caution mode, fire and reload, attack and guard against attacks. This is quite distinct from the fact that he can access an item menu and a map of the city. Through all the possible actions, the gamer—to repeat the terms describing the action tendency—can initiate, maintain, or alter his relationship with the hostile town of Silent Hill. The gameplay intensifies the emotional experience.

As with the circumstances of arousal of artifact emotions, the gameplay emotions rest on notions of control. Torben Grodal observes in "Video Games and the Pleasures of Control":

> Besides the central interface that controls perception and action, the games typically possess a series of additional control devices, from being able to choose several levels of difficulty, to time out features and the possibility of saving a positive intermediate result. Video games are therefore often "mood managers"; that is, they allow the player to participate in a self-controlled arousing experience. (2000, 209)

The game settings of *Silent Hill* allow, for instance, the usual configuration of difficulty levels (except for *SH: Origins* and *SH: Shattered Memories*). *SH1*, *SH2*, *SH3*, and *SH4: The Room* give you the choice between three levels (easy, normal, and hard). *SH: Homecoming* limits itself to two levels (normal and hard). Even though the game scenarios and endings are the same (instruction manual), you can select the action and riddle levels at the beginning of *SH2* and *SH3*.[5] Among other features in *SH2* and *SH3*, you can also choose between a 2-D camera-relative or a 3-D character-relative control type. In all the games, you can choose between different controller configurations. Quite meaningfully in survival horror games, the brightness level of the screen in all games can be adjusted (from 1 to 7, or darker to brighter). While the tailoring of the settings manages the relation between challenge, control preferences, and personal liking for adventure or/and action, the games themselves "are built to make it possible for players to gain control over the elicited arousal" (Grodal 2000, 209).

> The experience of given situations will change over time, due to learning processes which will change arousal and will change the cognitive labelling of the arousal. The emotional experience is not primarily input-

driven, arousal-driven, but driven by the wish for an active control, and thereby also driven by a wish for emotional control. (207)

Carrying on with his examination of the question of learning, Grodal describes the video game aesthetic as an *aesthetic of repetition* because the gamer has to understand, by repetitive rehearsal, how to cope with the game world and its inhabitants (2003, 148). He shows that the video game learning curve is similar to that of everyday experience: first the distress of unfamiliarity, then mastery, and finally automation. Indeed, at first, a game poses a challenge; it is unfamiliar and mysterious. But the more you play the game and become at ease with the controls, the more the system becomes familiar and the game world known. This leads, if not to total mastery, to a certain degree of control over the actions. You can start to predict what will happen next. Some actions you have to accomplish, some challenges you have to take up, and some problems you must face can turn into simple routines when you have a clear image of the gameplay patterns. For example, in order to make the possessed Cybil empty the magazine of her handgun at you at the merry-go-round of the amusement park in *SH1*, you must go behind the horse where she is sitting while the roundabout is in motion. When the roundabout stops, Cybil gets down and shoots at you but always hits the horse. You then have to run until the merry-go-round starts to move again and Cybil ends up on another horse. You can repeat this action pattern quite safely until the last bullet is fired. But once you learn to entirely control the situation, the challenge and suspense of these boss fights are gone.

The terror, fear, fright, dread, and panic provoked by *Silent Hill* are sharper and more intense the first time you step in. To catch up with the notions of online perception (vs. a leisurely analysis) and Grodal's game as an experiential route (vs. game as a map and as a system) as delineated in the introduction, the study of gameplay emotions created by survival horror needs to focus primarily on the initial phase of the learning sequence. It also has to give careful consideration to all aspects of gameplay. As Tosca remarks, rather pertinently, after having defined the plot and action levels:

> When we say that both levels are "active" in our minds at the same time, we don't mean that they are as clearly separated as here. This is an abstraction necessary for this analysis, but in fact the act of playing is more than a sum of the two, since actual gameplay is full of doubts, inef-

fective movement, reloads, maybe deaths, etc. This superfluous material is also part of playing, in a way it constitutes the act of playing. It is both informed by what we as players think that we have to do, our filling in-the-plot-gaps, and our playing ability (for example with the controllers in order to move, shoot, etc.). (2003, 211–12)

This is why we need to talk about gameplay emotions, and not game emotions.[6]

Welcome (We_com_) to *Silent Hill*!

Reviewers make frequent reference to the ending when critically appraising story-driven video games. Multiple endings being a feature that adds to the replay value, it is these last sequences that are most talked about, and *Silent Hill* has this attraction. However, the beginning of a game is as, if not more, important. Along with the demo, gamers choose to carry on playing a title after having gone through the first level, stage, or sequence. To reiterate Bordwell and Thompson's statement about films (1990, 62), a game does not just start, it *begins*. Both at the plot and action levels, the opening sets up a specific range of possible actions and outcomes. For example, some games like *Parasite Eve II* (Squaresoft / Squaresoft 2000) make you develop some skills by putting you through a training level before letting you go further. Others, in ways analogous to *Silent Hill*, make you jump in *in media res*. In any case, the events at the start of a game remain a privileged part since it is at this moment that you enter into a particular gaming experience. And the ways *SH1*, *SH2*, and *SH3* begin are indeed unrivaled,[7] while *SH: Homecoming* follows the path of the first and third games.

Aside from a reference to the quiet desolation into which the resort town of Silent Hill has slipped, to the memories of a tragic fire seven years ago, and to the car trouble leading Harry and Cheryl to arrive at night on the outskirts of the town they've come to for a late vacation, the prologue found in the *SH1* instruction manual summarizes the opening cut-scene and states the objective of the game in a straightforward manner: "Find Harry's missing daughter, Cheryl." When you begin your search after Harry wakes up in his vehicle, you find your inventory completely empty. Since Harry is not a member of a Special Tactics Force, he does not even have a combat knife to start the game (as does Chris in *Resident Evil* for instance). You do not have a map of this place either (but you know there is one by the manual). After the two short cut-scenes that direct you to the alley behind the figure of Cheryl, you follow the path. After it gets dark and Harry takes a match to light his way, you end up in front of a crucified body, and face to face with a pair of little monsters. If you succeed in getting Harry to elude these two demonic children, others are waiting to jump on him. Panic-stricken, you have no choice but to run and try to leave. But this alley will literally be a dead end: Harry will be killed further on. Thus, the first time you play *SH1*, you curse the game at once and wonder what the hell you'll have to do to escape those demonic children. Although you could assume that since Harry is holding a match, it would be surprising that he could use a weapon at the same time, you might think you missed a weapon along the way. If you did not try to go back to the alley you've just come through after it gets dark, you might believe there is a way out. This ratiocination lasts precisely seven seconds, which is the time the black screen loads and is followed, not by the usual "game over," but by the next "opening" cut-scene, where Harry wakes up with a start in the Cafe 5to2. At this moment, you realize that the first action you had to perform in *SH1* was indeed to get killed. That's quite an odd, remarkable, and unique introduction for a *survival* horror game. From the outset, you sit up and take notice. You grasp that the experiential route will be different.

SH3 is connected with *SH1* not only through its plots and its characters, but also through its beginning. The prologue in the instruction manual is more obtuse. Although it talks about the shopping mall and a chat on the phone, the description is more about the plunge into a new dimension. It states that Heather's "entire world was transformed into a grotesque and bizarre nightmare" and that she "was trapped alone in a deranged world, with nothing to do but escape. Not knowing where to turn, her only thought was of survival. She clutched her pistol tightly, ready to shoot anything that tried to attack." It therefore makes sense that Heather begins her journey in a nightmarish place, be it the Lakeside Amusement Park or a shopping mall. However, if Heather is surprised to find a knife in her hand at the start, it's also surprising for you to find a full inventory. Sure, you already have the trademark devices of *Silent Hill*, that is, the flashlight and the pocket radio, but you're also equipped with one health drink and one first-aid kit, along with a good set of weapons to choose from: the knife, a steel pipe, a loaded handgun (plus 30 more bullets), and a loaded submachine gun. The game might well start *in media res*, but that's not the start *SH1* and *SH2* taught you. After an exploration of the entrance of the amusement park, if you do not fall in a gaping hole in the floor, you go to a second area where you already have to face two monsters—a Double Head and a Closer. You might visit the souvenir shop before moving to an additional locale watched over by another Closer and finally to a third area where a Double Head and a Pendulum are waiting for you. Once you reach the bottom of the long stairway that leads to the roller coaster, you are prompted to follow the path until the boarding platform, and then go on the rails. While you might wonder where this will guide you, a cut-scene is triggered and a coaster comes to run over Heather. Inasmuch as the collision takes place off-screen and is staged in a cut-scene, you are just waiting for what is coming next. Once again, like her father, Heather wakes up from a nightmare in the Happy Burger. Your inventory has been emptied and now contains only a house key, a pendant, and a knife. But compared to *SH1*'s beginning, you had to explore more areas and play up to 15 or 20 minutes before finding out about the "nightmare" trick. You were prompted to think that you already started the game. With monsters to face from the outset, the in-game prologue (omitted when you start another new game) asserts that *SH3* is up for more action. And this is not a misconception.

SH: Homecoming extends on *SH3*'s opening. After the gurney ride presented in a cut-scene, the "X" button appears on the right corner of the screen to press you to free Alex from his straps and start to escape from the Alchemilla Hospital. Even though the level is named "Nightmare" when you save, you are incited to think this is already the first part of the game, the true beginning of your journey and not just a dream. Before Alex leaves the hospital, you'll do everything you usually do in a *Silent Hill* game. For instance, you have to search for one half of an X-Ray film to get the code to the security gate behind which Alex's young brother Joshua is awkwardly playing. As for Cheryl, Josh is running away from you. To try to get close to him again, you need to find his toy (the small bunny of *SH3*). Following the double nature of the resort town, the world turns to its nightmarish version when Alex finds a combat knife in the Women's Rest Room. The Nurses will then appear and attack him. If you die during a fight or by not getting your arm free fast enough from a hole in a wall, the game will start again at a save point as usual. Because you play around for a good hour, you come to forget that this might be another dimension. It is only when Alex is stricken by the Pyramid Head's great knife between the doors of the hospital elevator he finally reaches, but suddenly wakes up in the passenger seat of a truck on his way to Shepherd's Glen, that you're also realize that, again, you're welcomed into Silent Hill through a nightmare.

The beginning of *SH2* is the opposite of both *SH3* and *SH: Homecoming*. Its instruction manual's prologue presents, forthwith, the emotional instability of James, noting his "constant state of mourning" since the death of his wife Mary three years ago. Before the first cut-scene in front of Toluca Lake expands the description, the manual shortly discloses the letter signed by Mary in order to set off the objective of the game: you have to uncover the truth about the letter ("Mary . . . Could you really be in this town?"). Otherwise, the written introduction in the manual describes why James had to take a road in the forest to get to Silent Hill and the reason he finds himself in the run-down restroom where the game begins. With the map of the town found in the car, you only have the picture of Mary and her letter (which slowly disappears as the game goes on) in your inventory. To reach the town, you have to walk down a trail in the forest. You hear a monster roar, but it never comes out to attack you. After a while, you come across a well, which turns out to be a save point. As I have stated in the previous chapter, you move on with some hesitation. However, upon your entrance in the graveyard, you still do not face a monster although you might anticipate such encounter. Instead, you meet the harmless Angela in a cut-scene. Leaving the woman to her own search after a short chat, you exit the graveyard and walk along another trail that merges with Wiltse Road running along a dry river canal. When you finally reach Sanders Street, guided by large smears of blood on the roadway, you are prompted to chase after a figure that draws you toward a construction zone at the end of Vachss Road. Your investigation finally leads you to the first confrontation of the game. In the final analysis, when one does the calculation, it takes 16½ minutes if you walk and about 10 minutes if you run straight ahead to the end of Vachss Road before you face your first monster. Not to mention the usual searching and wandering which stretches out time, this is a very long time in a survival horror game. As this comment of *PlayStation2Era.com* exemplifies, one does not wonder why many reviews have underlined and criticized the pace of *SH2*:

> Let me begin by mentioning *SH2* is a slow game to get into. It takes about two hours for some real action to begin, and quite frankly I don't want to play a game that progresses like a turtle. By the time I had reached my

second hour, I lost all interest I had in playing *Silent Hill 2*. The game began to feel like a chore and a tedious adventure. (Katayev 2001)

The pace of the game is indeed acknowledged by the director Masashi Tsuboyama:

> At the beginning of the game we deliberately made the descent through the forest towards the cemetery longer. It's so long you don't feel like turning back. At the same time, it makes you realize just how totally isolated the city is ... and you also! We knew it was a bit risky in terms of gameplay, but we really wanted to take our chances and do it. (Beuglet 2001)

The risk was worth taking. Besides, this was not only taken for the first descent through the forest, but for many parts of the game. This daring shaped the gameplay of *SH2* as it will be discussed later in the chapter.

Have You Got the Key?

Introduced in the second chapter in regards to the plot and Carroll's curiosity theory, the concept of play of ratiocination becomes fundamental here. Insofar as a problem-solving structure can be seen as "the most reliable and effective way of generating intense emotional response in movie audiences" and as "the most economical framework for dishing up emotionally charged events" (Eitzen 1999, 88),[8] video games undeniably ask for a good play of ratiocination. You have to do more than anticipate what will happen next. Gameplay is about executing actions and solving puzzles. You can be perplexed about what's really happening in Silent Hill, or about the interpretation of an event or element, and still keep going. But you cannot remain confused in front of a locked door at the risk of being stopped and stuck there. As Murray has pointed out, "Computer-based journey stories offer a new way of savouring [the] pleasure [of answering a riddle], a pleasure that is intensified by uniting the problem solving with the active process of navigation" (1997, 139).

The gameplay of *Silent Hill* is typical of the survival horror genre. While facing impure monsters or a possible threat, you have to (1) discover ways to get to places while roads are blocked, (2) locate keys to unlock doors, (3) find items to get those keys, and (4) solve puzzles to know how to get those items/keys and how to move on. For example, in *SH1*, you have to deduce the actions to perform at the normal Midwich Elementary School after reading three notes written in blood linked to time, that is, to the Clock Tower of the Courtyard guarded by little monsters:

10:00 *"Alchemy laboratory"* Gold in an old man's palm. The future hidden in his fist. Exchange for sage's water.
[Get the "chemical" (concentrated hydrochloric acid) in the Lab Equipment Room. Use it on the statue of an old man's hand in the Chemistry Lab to get the Gold medallion. Place it in the "Golden Sun" slot of the Clock Tower in order to make the hands stop at 12:00. Actually, as it was closed if you went before, this opens the piano's door in the Music Room.]

12:00 *"A place with songs and sound."* A silver guidepost is untapped in lost tongues. Awakening at the ordained order.
[Go to the Music Room. Read the poem written in blood ("A tale of birds without a voice") to know how to play the dead notes in the right order. Get the Silver medallion. Place it in the "Silver Moon" slot of the Clock Tower in order to make the hands stop at 5:00.]

5:00 *"Darkness that brings the choking heat."* Flames render the silence, awakening the hungry beast. Open time's door to beckon prey.
[Go to the Boiler Room in the basement. Switch it on. Go back to the Clock Tower. Enter it.]

Depending on the level of difficulty chosen in *SH2* and *SH3*, the game's riddles are simplified and hints are provided. Some puzzle's solutions, like codes to open boxes, are randomly generated in the two games. But as the above example leads you to understand, there are many gatherings in *Silent Hill*. This is not to mention the various items you need to find in order to combine them. Analogous to the collection of crests in *Resident Evil*, you have to find four Plates to cross a door in the nightmarish Alchemilla Hospital of *SH1*, and five different items in "Nowhere" to proceed to the final boss fight, whereas it is five Tarot Cards that allow you to unlock this last door in *SH3*. In *SH2*, you need to get three coins to earn a key in the Blue Creek Apartment, three Tablets in the Toluca Prison for a Horseshoe, and three Music Boxes for the important Stairway Key of the Lake View Hotel. In *SH: Homecoming,* five Plates have to be found and put in the pentagon's slots of the church's organ in order to open a secret chamber. To help you find them, the player character turns his head to look at interesting items during his search. But contrary to *Resident Evil,* the backtracking is quite limited in *Silent Hill*. The search and the use of items are limited to a rather specific area, and the maps are automatically annotated in red to let you know where you've been. For instance, if you visit the Music Room at the school ahead of time, the location of the piano is immediately noted on the map, giving you a clue about its importance. Then, as previously mentioned, the Horseshoe is to be combined with a Wax Doll and Lighter in order to make a handle to open a trapdoor; they are all found in the Toluca Prison. Moreover, the items (like any others that need such operations) are placed next to each other in the inventory, which encourages you to think about combining them. This is also true for items that have to be used one after the other, like the jack to open the elevator doors on the third floor of the normal Hilltop Center in *SH3* and the rope to climb down. By removing the monsters from the "real" world, *SH: Shattered Memories* emphasizes the exploration part of the journey. Since the items, hints, or keys are not far away from locked doors and new ways in the game, this journey becomes more of a crossing than a difficult systematic search. During the various frozen nightmares, the GPS map function of Harry's cell phone in *SH: Shattered Memories* keeps track of your moves and gives you some hints to help you escape the labyrinth and flee from the monsters.

Instead of the inventories of *Alone in the Dark* and *Resident Evil,* and with the exception of *SH4: The Room*, which has an item box in Henry's living room and a limitation on the items carried into the Otherworld, the inventory of Silent Hill is unlimited. You don't need to manage your inventory by dropping items or by storing them in boxes near save points in order to get them later. *Silent Hill* does not hinder your progress with this kind of juggling. In fact, this gaming trickery happens only once, and then it is carried to an extreme. At the Lake View Hotel in *SH2*, an alarm rings when you enter the Employee Elevator. A message written over the buttons indicates: "Weight allowance: one person." Consequently, you have to place all your items, down to the very last one, on the shelf next to the elevator. This means James has to move on completely without resources and utterly powerless. Since it is the first and only time you face such a situation, you become really anxious about what will happen next. When you return later, finding all your stuff brings a great relief.

Coping with the Resort Town

The gamer and the spectator are akin in the way that both are always aware they are not themselves the victim of the horror and that it is someone else suffering (as in Tan 1996, 241). This is the fictional dimension of the experience. But while, ideally, their emotional responses run parallel to those of the characters, their way of feeling tension, fear, and physical pain is different.

In a horror film, the emphasis is put on the characters' internal reactions to monsters, reactions Carroll best associates with the "behavioral" type:

> Just before the monster is visualized to the audience, we often see the characters shudder in disbelief, responding to this or that violation of nature. Their faces contort; often their noses wrinkle and their upper lip curls as if confronted by something noxious. They start backwards in a reflex of avoidance. Their hands may be drawn toward their bodies in an act of protection but also of revulsion and disgust. Along with fear of physical harm, there is an evident aversion to making physical contact with the monster. Both fear and disgust are etched on the characters' features. (1990, 22–23)

In fact, in specifying that the reaction is often seen through a close-up from a subjective point of view, this describes "one of the most frequent and compelling images in the horror film repertoire" (qtd. in Carroll 1990, 243 n. 45). Inasmuch as the characters in horror films exemplify, for the spectator, the manner in which to react to the monsters, the latter is also prompted to behave the same way. What's more, often shown in close shots and in shot/reverse-shot where both the point of view of the victim and the one of the monster are adopted, the spectator is forced to witness the bloody confrontations. On the brink of finding the action too scary, he or she can put his hands over his eyes to defend himself against the horrible vision (but one still hears what's going on).

Although cut-scenes can depict a horrible scene in a filmic way, a survival horror or terror game does not rest on the reports of characters' internal reactions. Indeed, the third-person perspective always shows the player character in a long or medium shot, and generally, in a long take too. To be able to face the monsters, the player character is furthermore seen from the back. There is no prior or subsequent reaction shot of a face expressing stark terror and attesting to the threat. The filmic subjective shot structure that makes you feel *as if* you were in the situation of a character is replaced here by the sense of agency. Janet Murray has defined this characteristic delight of electronic environments in *Hamlet on the Holodeck: The Future of Narrative in Cyberspace:* "Agency is the satisfying power to take meaningful actions and see the results of our decisions and choices" (1997, 126). You are in command of your player character in the game world, an ascendancy that leads to a mutation in the way you experience the scene. But this does not grant you total control. Giving advice about writing for horror games, Richard Dansky says: "One of the unspoken rules of horror games is that the player does not control the environment. They are constantly off-balance, reacting to the world with imperfect knowledge" (2009, 114). This is true of *Silent Hill*, where, as Inger Ekman and Petri Lankoski observe for *SH2*, "The whole game world breathes with life, suggesting that somehow the environment itself is alive, sentient, and capable of taking action against the player" (2009, 193). Imamura acknowledges this in an interview:

> CVG: What do you think you can offer with horror in a videogame that can't be offered with horror in a movie?
>
> AKIHIRO IMAMURA: The game medium is different from film in that you have interactivity. You will feel as if you're in a scene. For example, your main character is in the game. You know something is there but don't know what it is and you get scared. You tend to feel the fear; I'm pretty sure that you will feel much more intensity than you would by watching a movie. (CVG 2001)

It is certainly not the main character that is meant to be scared, but the gamer. If the reader recalls the second chapter comments on fiction emotions, it is even more clear here that one cannot talk about identification since the emotional state of the character is not identical to yours. Because, even though Travis, Harry (in both games), James, Heather, Henry, and Alex make themselves heard during their fight and breathe their last breath as Harry does, all remain impassive on the action level. Whatever the situation faced in Silent Hill, they keep a "stone face" while responding to actions.[9] Instead, their reactions are truly behavioral and external. You are linked with them physically. You see their actions and are made to feel their physical pain through the force feedback of the Dualshock controller. In *Silent Hill*, the controller vibrates characteristically when the player characters are touched or hit. It even does this when Harry charges into a wall or falls from house balconies in *SH1*, sufficiently so to make you jump if you don't pay close attention. Also, to indicate their health status, it also shakes more and more violently as they absorb more damage (following *SH2* and *SH3* instruction manuals), re-creating the acceleration of their heartbeat. These tactile simulations focus on physical strength for the simple reason that it helps you keep them alive. This is another departure for the video game.

In movies, Carroll says, "the fear that the audience emotes with regard to the monster is not fear for its own survival. Our fear is engendered in behalf of the human characters in the pertinent films. We cringe when the Werewolf of London stalks his prey, not because we fear that he'll trap us, but because we fear for some character in the film" (1999, 38). Again, you do not fear for your survival in a horror game. However, in the game world, since your repertoire of actions is that of the player characters', and since your main goal is precisely to make them survive Silent Hill, you're indeed made to be afraid that the monsters will trap you, to fear *as if* you were in danger. This time, when the action becomes really scary, you can't simply put your hand before your eyes. Holding your controller, your extradiegetic activity must be to try and overcome the diegetic situation.[10] While these actions are performed by pushing the buttons and manipulating the thumbsticks of the Playstation or Xbox controller, the combination of the nunchuk and the Wii remote of the Nintendo Wii console maps the actions a little bit more to the gamer's body in *SH: Shattered Memories*. For instance, you point the Wii remote toward the screen to aim the flashlight and thrust the two controllers in the direction of an attacking creature to shove it. But in accordance with John Morreal's observations about negative emotions (1985, 99), when the fear gets too strong, you lose control and can't direct your thoughts or actions. The Roach Trap in the sewers of the Historical Society Museum in *SH2* is built specifically to take advantage of your agitation, thus preventing you, for a moment, from thinking wisely. Surrounded by Roaches, you have to find a three-digit code on a nine-digit panel in order to get out. If it seems at first that you will have to trust your luck, you soon realize after a few tries that two or three digits are lit up and you only have to combine these to get out. Conversely, and somewhat more frequently in *SH3*—which is aiming, says scenario writer Owaku, to provoke a "more violent, direct feeling of fear" (Beuglet 2003)—getting in dark places filled with monsters waiting to attack just makes you go to pieces and run in panic.

What Imamura implies about fear ("I'm pretty sure that you will feel much more intensity than you would by watching a movie"), Torben Grodal elucidates with great clarity.

> The player's emotional experience is a personalized one. When a viewer is observing, say, how a monster is approaching a character, the possible arousal in the form of fear is not linked to the personal coping potential of the viewer, the viewer has to vicariously identify with the coping potentials of the endangered film character. The viewer cannot

personally come up with specific coping strategies; like the rest of the audience, the viewer can only hope for a positive outcome and eventually make some more personal predictions. But a player of a video game is personally responsible for the outcome of such a confrontation. It is the player's evaluation of his own coping potential that determines whether the confrontation with a monster will be experienced as fear (if the evaluation of his coping potential is moderate), despair (if he feels that he has no coping potentials), or triumphant aggression (if he feels that he is amply equipped for the challenge). This entails that the emotional experience will vary over time, due to the learning processes leading to a change in coping potentials. (2003, 150)

Your active coping potentials derive from many aspects of *Silent Hill*. From the outset, there isn't a Panic Meter as in *Clock Tower 3* that sees the player character (Alyssa) acting increasingly erratically as it rises to the point where she is not responding to your commands anymore. Nor is there a Sanity Meter as in *Eternal Darkness: Sanity's Requiem* (Silicon Knights / Nintendo 2002) which, once it falls very low, makes weird things happen to your player characters, game world, television set, and console. On the other hand, the controls of *Silent Hill* are quite imperfect. Although this flaw is one of the main complaints about the series, it is nonetheless part of the game.

> While fixed camera angles, dodgy controls and clunky combat were seen as problematic in most games, the traditional survival horror took them as a positive boon. A seemingly less demanding public ate up these games with a big spoon, overlooking glaring faults in favor of videogames that could be genuinely terrifying.
>
> Up until the PlayStation 2 era, it was a formula for success, arguably perfected by the brilliant *Silent Hill 2*. Restricted cameras caused players to fear every step they took, while characters that couldn't hold a gun steady encouraged players to flee rather than fight. (Sterling 2008)

One hint found in the *SH1* instruction manual (repeated for that matter in *SH2*'s manual with slight changes) reflects on the formula and applies it for the whole series: "Since the character is a normal person with no special training in shooting a gun, his skill with it is marginal. Even in daylight or with the flashlight on, his accuracy with the weapon is questionable [from which the auto-aim facing a monster] and is certainly dependent on the distance. Try to let the enemies close in a bit to get off a sure hit." Reviewers like *Gamespot*'s Lark Anderson (2008) might well have underlined that "as a soldier, Alex is gifted with a martial prowess and combat training that the other Silent Hill protagonists lacked," but *SH: Homecoming*'s player character is really not the "powerhouse in battle" that *Resident Evil 4*'s Leon S. Kennedy (Capcom / Capcom 2005) or *Resident Evil 5*'s (now all muscles) Chris Redfield (Capcom / Capcom 2005) is, and the Konami's gunplay does not have the new accuracy of Capcom's. In *Silent Hill*, the player characters do not run that fast either; they get out of breath while running, which slows them down (Heather is especially slow when she gets a heavy bulletproof vest). As Jim Sterling underlines, accepting these lapses in control, which make the player characters react to situations less than ideally and in ways you might react yourself—which might actually get you killed once in a while—brings out the best in the experience.

Another hint found in the *SH1* instruction manual (as in the *SH2* manual, yet with slight changes) gives a method to cope with the monsters that perfectly characterizes the gameplay of *Silent Hill*: "The creatures have eyes and ears and use these to locate the character. So if they are not alerted to the character's presence, they will not start attacking. NOTE: If the light is turned off and the character is careful not to go right in front of creatures, he can avoid needless confrontation." As you would do in real life, you can stand still in a corner when you see a monster or hear its presence and wait till the threat is gone. You can also progress slowly in the dark when you have plotted a path beforehand, or can take to your heels and run away. If this last solution is often one of the best in the streets, especially since the impure monsters of Silent Hill are known to not be particularly quick, it turns out to be an inefficient solution in a corridor. Whether or not you are a *killer* that envisages every single battle with a drive to kill and triumph, you need to confront and destroy monsters in Silent Hill as in any survival horror game (and as in any horror story, as Carroll would say). The end of the hint in the instruction manual puts it clearly: "It is not possible to complete the adventure with the light off" and totally avoid fighting. You cannot avoid the boss monsters. Along with good health, and the skills to move around (running away and quickly turning 180 degrees to face back enemy), the confrontations require appropriate weapons. The evaluation of your coping potential depends a great deal on those variables. While it can be hard to fight Slurpers crawling across the ground with melee weapons in *SH3*, being out of bullets becomes less stressful in the indoor locations of *SH1* from the moment you get the hammer or the bonus katana in a "Next fear" game. In any case, it's always reassuring to be able to rely on loaded guns in your inventory, be it a handgun, a shotgun, or a hunting rifle. Part of the pleasure of the games—except for *SH: Shattered Memories*, which doesn't include any weapon—rests on this arsenal and is advertised that way: "Battle grotesque monstrosities with all-new weapons, including a sub-machine gun and a katana" (*SH2* and *SH3* box set) or "Battle nightmarish creatures with an arsenal of deadly weapons" (*SH: Homecoming* box set). *SH: Origins* allows you to use many items as melee weapons, from a toaster to a typewriter, a light stand to a shovel. What's more, you can get bonus weapons throughout the series (and use them depending on your preferences): a rock drill, a chainsaw, a circular saw, a big butcher's cleaver, Lonely Moon Gauntlets, a hyper blaster, a hyper spray, a flamethrower, a submachine gun with unlimited ammunition, and, to introduce some sci-fi elements referring to the UFO ending, a beam saber, a Heather Beam, a Tesla Rifle, or a laser pistol.

Absolutely Terrified

Diane Carr (2006) distinguishes the horror fantasy role-playing game from the survival horror game. The former is configured as a tangled rhizome so encyclopedic and rambling that it defies resolution, comprehension, and totality. The latter is designed as a solvable maze,[11] sequential, linear, and its ability to generate tension and fright is fulfilled by its more directed gameplay. Although Carr's comparison adequately defines what *Silent Hill* is all about, the series has been criticized, far too often, for its linearity. Yet this is no sin, especially not regarding a story-driven game. Great games simply nudge you in the right direction without giving you the impression that you are only stringing together the story events. Moreover, *Silent Hill* often cleverly directs your action. The beginnings of *SH1* and *SH2*, described above, are good examples. Harry is guided by his daughter via short cutscenes, and James is led by marks of blood on the roadway representing some sort of "arrows" integrated into the game world. *SH3* has likewise gripping "guided ways." There is of course the Borley Haunted Mansion, which you do not cross without having some terrible fright and without having to face danger and run for your life. One also thinks about the long reddish, sinuous corridor in concrete Heather has to use on her way to the hellish Brookhaven Hospital to meet Leonard. Since ultimately this is not a labyrinth to get lost in or to face enemies in, you might just have to follow the path mapped out by the gates, which are rapidly closing and opening on your moves. But the loud metal noises of the gates piercing the silence, sometimes off-screen, are enough to alarm you and send chills down your spine. Finally, in this respect, it's hard to forget the train that takes Heather from Hazel Street to an unknown subway station. The train is running, so you can only go forward in a straight line. If you want to go back, you'll find yourself at the back of the train (in any car you are since these mysteriously disappear upon your crossing) and in danger of falling off. You therefore have to cross the eight cars, half of them lit, some of them guarded by five Numb Bodies and an Insane Cancer. The controller vibrates, so as to re-create the rolling on the rails, and you really feel *as if* you were in this "train from/to hell."

Though it lacks the openness of a role-playing game world, exploration is nonetheless at the heart of *Silent Hill*. Objecting to the distinction made by Marie-Laure Ryan in her online article (2001) between an exploratory mode of interactivity ("where the user is free to move around the database, but this activity does not make history nor does it alter the plot"), and an ontological one (where "the decisions of the user send the history of the virtual world on different forking paths"), Grodal explains that there is no clear distinction between exploring and altering a game world.[12] He then formulates a fundamental assertion:

> When I wander around in a mystery, adventure or a shoot-'em-up game, I cannot change the fundamental layout of the game-world just as I cannot change Italy by my visit, but nevertheless I control my navigation, my ability to shoot monsters, etc., and create many different stories. Thus, interactivity is not centrally about changing a world; on the contrary, it is about changing the mental states of the player, whether that takes place by changing some objects in the world or by changing one's point of view. (2003, 142)

If there is one thing that *Silent Hill* does masterfully, it is well and truly to change your mental state, to terrify you. Just think of the feeling evoked when the door of the cell where the "Tablet of The Oppressor" is in the Toluca prison seems to get stuck. I lose my head! Isn't it a real deliverance when the door opens and you can get out of the tiny and dreary space?!

Both on the riddle level, already addressed early on, and the action level, the exploration of *Silent Hill* shapes the game experience. As it was noted in the preceding chapter, the meticulous design of the resort town renders the visit a riveting one. You can therefore take what I have called in the introduction the attitude of a *player* and just wander around, not so much to find information as to see what type of stores can be found on a street, or what is hanging on the walls in the indoor locations. Of course you cannot as easily go for a ramble in Silent Hill. Many streets are blocked. What is most important is the fact that you feel like you are under surveillance in those streets and places. When impure monsters (and not cops or guards as in action games) are stalking you, possibly waiting at every street corner or behind every door in order to attack you, the stroll is somewhat less nonchalant. The ability to act within and upon the world is certainly one important form of agency, and a great source of pleasure. But as the survival horror genre emphasizes, one gets as much emotion from the power to *act upon* as from the possibility of *being acted upon*. Thus the "rush" you get during the fight.

With such threats always hanging over you, you better watch your step. As in *Alone in the Dark* and *Resident Evil*, Team Silent and their followers are having fun startling you. Following the example of monsters breaking through windows or zombies coming out of closets in *Resident Evil*, an Insane Patient suddenly jumps out from under a truck at the beginning of *SH2*, and a Sleeper from under the bed in a room of Onestop in the nightmarish Hilltop Centre of *SH3*. Followed by a hanging corpse, a piece of metal furniture suddenly falls down noisily from the ceiling right in front of Alex in one of the dark corridors of the Alchemilla Hospital at the beginning of *SH: Homecoming*. Without a doubt, scripted events are wonderful vehicles for these types of intense automatic emotional responses. In accordance with Robert Baird's analysis, the game designers have the core elements of the film threat scene's startle effect at their disposal:

> (1) a character presence, (2) an implied offscreen threat, and (3) a disturbing intrusion [accentuated by sound bursts] into the character's immediate space. This is the essential formula (character, implied threat, intrusion) one finds repeated hundreds and thousands of times since Lewton's first bus effect [in Jacques Tourneur's *Cat People*, produced by Val Lewton in 1942]. (2000, 15)

Baird gives as an example a threat scene in *Alien* (Ridley Scott, 1979), where Ripley (Sigourney Weaver) and two of her teammates, thinking the beast hides inside, carefully open a locker, only to be surprised by an extreme close-up of a shrieking cat jumping out, its every movement frenzied (2000, 18). There are two similar scenes in the locker room of *SH1*'s Midwich Elementary School. I referred to the first one in the third chapter; as you approach a series of boxes where you hear something or someone begging to be let out, a cut-scene quickly makes a cat spring out of the box in a shock cut at the very moment Harry is about to open it. There is no close-up, but you're still startled! The second scene, dependent upon this first one, takes place in the nightmarish world. You hear the same banging and still get close to a box, from which, this time, blood drips out. A cut-scene stages Harry moving his hand to open the box, but nothing happens. The box opens itself and there is nothing inside. Regaining the control over Harry in a high-angle shot from the ceiling, you begin to leave when, in a shock cut and a shock vibration on the controller, a body suddenly falls down from a locker in a close, low-angle shot that does not have the usual letterbox format of the cut-scenes. Like the famous bus scene from *Cat People* Baird talks about, where the threat is evoked from the left of the female character while a bus barrels in from the right of the screen, the scene catches you off guard. The same thing happens in *SH2* when Maria, whom you've just left in the reception office of Brookhaven Hospital, is suddenly next to the typewriter in the small document room. The shock of her apparition is intensified by a change of shot, but even more by her sudden illumination from James's flashlight (fig. 11).

This is not the only time this kind of apparition will make you jump. Insofar as it needs an implied off-screen threat and a disturbing intrusion into the character's immediate space, the flashlight in itself gives rise to startle effects. A controllable framing within the frame of the screen, its light beam doubles the effect of the off-s(cr)een. It literally creates a play between the seen and the unseen, between light and darkness (especially with a low brightness level). Akin to the Double Head that springs up in front of Heather at the top of a staircase in the metro station, at first, you only see dark silhouettes that often enter your field of vision. To be able to kill the monsters, you need to see them, to light them. When you come face to face with a monster at the turn of a corridor, you may jump with fright because the trail of the beam of light makes you meet not only an ugly figure, but a strikingly bright one in the dark.

On the level of sound, I have already noted the noises suddenly bursting in rooms. A particular sudden bang on the door at the back of the clothing store where you get the bulletproof vest is also unnerving in *SH3*. Since you

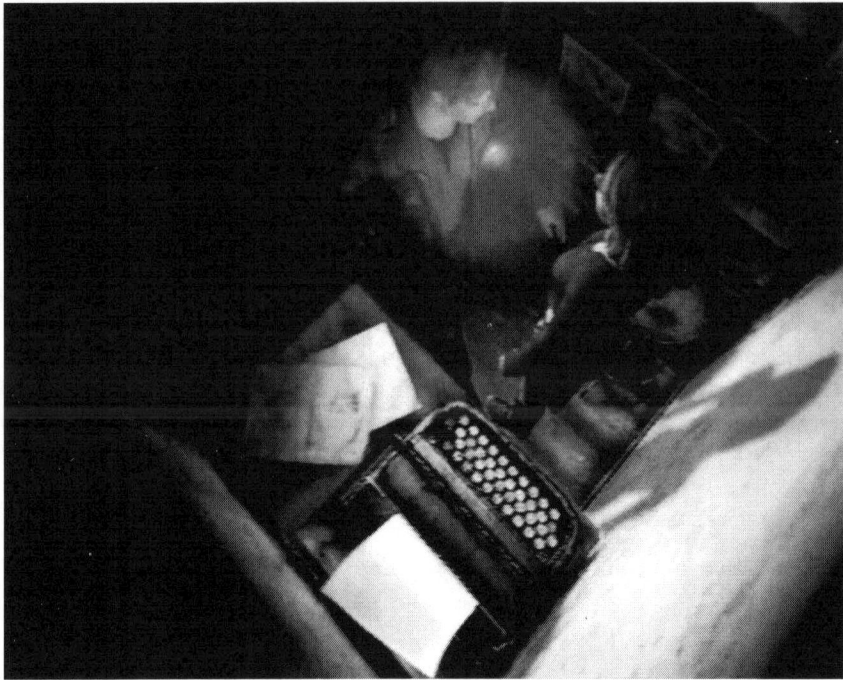

Fig. 11. *Silent Hill 2*: Maria making a sudden apparition next to the typewriter in the small document room of Brookhaven Hospital

can only see in front of you with the flashlight, you hurriedly look around to see what made that noise and if a monster is there. What's more, when you are made aware of the threat from the left, the right, or behind you, you become conscious of the use of surround sound and of the 360-degree space of the video game. You truly look around.

Governed by its atmosphere rather than its action, *Silent Hill* does not assault you as aggressively as *Resident Evil*. With its innovative use of audiovisual devices, the series designs a visceral experience that is, as it is exposed, more psychological. The startle effect or sudden surprise is at one end of a spectrum where the other end is constituted by "higher" emotions—"complex mixtures of temporal situation, cognitive appraisal, physiological response, and conscious feelings" (Plantinga 1995). In this perspective, *Silent Hill* exploits to its advantage other approaches to inducing fear responses. In a study about the "effect of forewarning on emotional responses to a horror film," Joanne Cantor, Dean Ziemke, and Glenn G.

Sparks show that one would intuitively think that prior knowledge about an upcoming frightening event would reduce its emotional impact by reducing the degree of uncertainty about what will happen. On the contrary, the notion "forewarned is forearmed" does not lead to "emotional defences" or effective coping strategy so much as a buildup of lasting arousal prior to the event (1984, 22–23). Using heart rate as the measure of physiological arousal, and describing in more or less detail the events forthcoming in four vampire scenes, Cantor, Ziemke. and Sparks asked the subjects of their experiment to rate their anxiety, fright, and upset[13] with regard to the scenes. Their answers resulted in the following observation:

> Forewarning of upcoming events did the opposite of "forearming" subjects against emotional reactions. Subjects who were given prior knowledge of upcoming frightening events reported more intense fright and upset in response to the movie than did those who had no forewarning.
>
> It is interesting to note that reports of fright and upset were intensified by forewarning, but reports of anxiety were not. As will be recalled, fright and upset were expected to reflect responses to specific depicted or anticipated events, whereas anxiety was presumed to denote an uneasiness over uncertain outcomes. Given that forewarning should have decreased rather than increased uncertainty, it does not seem surprising that anxiety ratings were not increased by forewarning. (1984, 30)

These conclusions help to explain why the visceral experience of *Silent Hill* is more intricate than mere automatic response, more about terror than (art-)horror as it was distinguished in the first chapter. Travis, Harry, James, Heather, and Alex, of course, carry a great forewarning tool. The pocket radio is a fundamental element of the games. While a few reviewers have suggested turning it off (in order to have an experience like that in *Resident Evil*), it seems better to follow the *SH2* manual's advice: "The monsters cannot hear the radio noise, so turning it off would be foolish." Every time it starts to transmit white noise so as to warn you that one or many monsters are nearby, you take fright at what you'll be confronting, and this heightens awareness of the encounter. Without doubt, your heart rate will accelerate (one can only wonder what Cantor, Ziemke, and Sparks's experiment conducted with survival horror games would have given as a result). Yet, contrary to Cantor, Ziemke, and Sparks's forewarning, which precisely describes the frightening event,[14] the pocket radio of *Silent Hill* signifies a threat, but does not reveal anything regarding what is about to occur. There still remains an uneasiness over the uncertainty of the outcome. Thus, not only fright, but anxiety too is intensified. Because you feel *as if* you are in the game world and the threat is directed at you, event-induced emotions are felt with even more intensity.

There are many moments where the radio's forewarning, combined with the sound design and the darkness, engenders arousal. To give some examples from my own experience of the first games, I was always taking cover when the pocket radio informed me of the presence of a Flying Reptile at the beginning of *SH1*. Running feverishly under the trees on the sidewalk of Ellroy Street to avoid an aerial attack, I stopped after a turn on Finney Street because I was hearing the white noise again. While I was waiting, thinking I was safe under the tree, I realized that the reptile I was expecting was in fact hidden just above my head. I decamped rather rapidly. I was also driven by fear in the Dark West South Vale of *SH2* while the radio was emitting its alarm and an unseen monster screamed at me when I turned the corner of Monson Street and Nathan Avenue. I ran with even more compulsion upon catching a glimpse of the noisy Patient Demon just before I reached Rosewater Park. Oddly enough, for a certain time I was of two minds as to how to get out of the laundry room on the third floor of *SH2*'s Wood Side Apartments. Hearing the white noise, footsteps of some sort, and what seemed to be the growl and shrieking of a huge monster, I was too scared to move. When I finally came out, I was very tensed up, anticipating an encounter, with what turned out to be no more than a lone Patient Demon. A situation like this gives you the creeps because it illustrates how *Silent Hill* is playing with you and, to use Imamura's terms, building the feeling of fear little by little. The penetrating, sped-up respiration of the Nurses when you get in the Brookhaven Hospital in *SH2* is a good illustration. They seem to follow close on your heels, but are, in reality, far off. The emotional impact is more intense at the end of the elevator ride that leads Heather to the nightmarish side of the Centre Square Shopping Centre in *SH3*. In pitch-black corridors, intermittently lit with only a few fluorescent ceiling lights (the flashlight not being found yet), I was really thrown into panic by the omnipresent loud growls, howls, and noises of torn flesh. Since the door of the first-aid room, the only one unlocked in this section of the center, is in a dark corner, I ran, only to face the Double Heads. At one point it was only by firing of my handgun that I was able to see that only one Double Head, and not many, was waiting in front of a door. It was only later that I came to understand that the Double Heads made those fearsome noises because they were eating chunks of flesh, not because they were after me. These are the moments I may not have underlined enough in studying the forewarning system in the survival horror genre (Perron 2004). According to Guillaume Roux-Girard, "However, what Perron fails to highlight is that forewarning does not rely only on the sound function of the same name. To be really effective, the forewarning must be unreliable and/or the quantity of information about the localisation of the generator [of the sound] must be limited" (Roux-Girard 2010, 205). To create its terrifying atmosphere, *Silent Hill* is indeed frequently "luring the gamer with sound," a sound strategy of survival horror games studied by Roux-Girard.

If the signified presence of the monsters and their eventual assaults are mainly responsible for your fear and apprehension, *Silent Hill* purposely develops what we can call—following yet another psychological account of the video game—an exploration anxiety. Here you do not have to cope with enemies, your stock of ammunitions, or your combat skills; you have to deal with your memory. Hayden Duvall illustrates how a gamer, dropped into a strange new environment, can feel confused, and how the huge amount of important information to memorize in a free exploration can make him unable to remember whether or not he has been down a particular path and thus become unsure about which direction to take.[15] Whereas Duvall studies these memory-related problems to show that they can considerably reduce a gamer's enjoyment, there is no choice but to accept that these actually accomplish the reverse in *Silent Hill*. The games have a good map system, and this is not without reason. Howard Grossman says in the *SH: Origins Official Strategy Guide:* "The map feature is so critical in this game that it is given its own button on the controller" (2007, 6). Dan Birlew gives similar advice in the *Silent Hill 2 Official Strategy Guide:* "The map is your key to geographical orientation. . . . Often as you go around town, you won't be able to remember which direction you're going or even what street you're on. Even after several games, it's still easy to get lost. It's the disorienting effect of the game—it is *supposed* to happen" (2001, 23). Indeed, Team Silent and, after them, the designers at Double Helix Games and Climax Studios have understood that by getting you lost, they'll put you in a position where you'll be more deeply overcome with fear. Alone in the dark, you definitely come to wonder how you're going to escape this hell. This proves to be even worse when you "don't have the map for this area or place" (onscreen notification), and you cannot find it anywhere. This happens in *SH1*. Taking the elevator down in the Alchemilla Hospital actually brings you to a place called "Nowhere." In *SH: Shattered Memories*, Harry jumps down twice to such "Nowhere" labyrinthine levels at the exit of the pawnshop. The beginning of the second level even has glass or invisible walls in which the outlines need to be traced with the flashlight. After all you've been through, you have to make the final stretch using your own sense of orientation. You have to do the same in the Lakeside Amusement Park of *SH3*. With a slight change, consisting of a map drawn as you explore the place, you have to grope your way through the Church at the end of *SH3* and through the Labyrinth of *SH2*. Again, it's quite disturbing to find yourself confronting a blank space (literally and figuratively), and not knowing where you're going. The warp doors that suddenly transport you to another room are also disorientating. This is the case with a few rooms of the nightmarish Lake View Hotel (as Room 202 transports you outside Room 219 on the other side of the hotel) and of the girls' restrooms of the alternate Midwich Elementary School of *SH1*. You can become really baffled trying to find out that you no longer have access to the corridor when you exit the restroom. This is before you realize that the restrooms act as an elevator between the first (1F) and the second (2F) floors. Here you can rely on the map, but it is not possible to do the same in the "Nowhere" level, where an important warp door also acts as stairs between the first and second floors.

A Last Stretch of Time

It is impossible to bring the discussion to a close without talking about the particularities of *SH2*'s gameplay. As I have stated, speaking of the beginning, the director, Masashi Tsuboyama, points out that Team Silent has taken an important risk regarding gameplay, which is what makes it such an exceptional game.

SH2 is very slow paced. It is not an action-filled package. The monsters are not that numerous and are easily avoided. In fact, *SH2* relies on one of the most essential features of gameplay: time, real time. It is indicative of the way you are made to play the game that you simply can't kill Pyramid Head. You can only endure through enough time to make him leave or kill himself (or themselves when a second Pyramid Head appears at the end). Along with the lengthy descent through the forest, certain sequences that might seem overlong are inserted deliberately to convey a feeling of isolation (Beuglet 2001). The more you go on, descending into the abyss of the resort town, the longer become the transitions (stairways, corridors, and walks in the streets) to new places or locations. It should be repeated, one last time, that you feel totally alone in the dark of Silent Hill. When you leave the nightmarish Brookhaven Hospital after the first death of Maria, you have to "follow the map," that is, get a letter and a wrench on Lindsey Street, then go back to Rosewater Park in order to get a key to the Silent Hill Historical Society Museum, your final destination. Although you can stop (again) in the Motorhome on Saul Street (the last save point before the museum) and at Neely's Bar on Neely Street, running to Lindsey Street still takes you around nine minutes, when all you have to do is steer clear of Demon Patients. Getting to the park, free of enemies, and searching for the key might take you another 10 minutes. Then, with no ellipse teleporting you there, you have to run all the way to the Museum on Nathan Avenue (anyone still walking at this stage?!). After your long, urban ride, the three minutes or so that it takes to cover the distance are unnerving. With the sidewalk changing to grass, the guardrails, and the total obscurity of whatever is off the road, you realize you are leaving town. So if you did not quite feel safe in the city, there is really nothing reassuring about a walk to Silent Hill's outskirts. Many horror scenes have taken place in remote places.

At the museum, at the call of what sounds like a boat's foghorn, you have to go down a narrow, dark, tight, steep stairway (there are similar ones in the subway section of *SH3;* you go down a long staircase as well to face Travis's daddy in *SH: Origins* and another one to jump to Nowhere in *SH: Shattered Memories*). You run down and down, but the stairs seem to be never-ending. In fact, roughly one long minute is necessary to reach the next door. I stopped twice on my way down. While James was out of breath the first time, I guess I was suffocating. Totally immersed in the game world, I was seized with a dread of being trapped. Despite the fact that I've never been claustrophobic in everyday life, I really got a bad feeling in this stairway. My apprehension was at its peak. Even though I cannot say if he is also talking about this particular moment, Christophe Gans, the French filmmaker who directed the *Silent Hill* movie, points out another dimension of such transitions.

> The abnormal duration of this sequence literally carries you to the edge of panic. In general, the player seeks the *addiction,* the dependence on the game; in no case does he want to be confronted with the certainty of not doing anything. Then Silent Hill brings him back to the idea of duration, and somewhere to the pathos of his condition. (Higuinen and Tesson 2002b, 31; my translation)

Fig. 12. *Silent Hill 2*: James Sunderland crossing Toluca Lake to reach the Lake View Hotel

The notion of duration cannot be overlooked with regard to the crossing of the Toluca Lake either. You have to row the boat across the lake to reach the Lake View Hotel. Without the help of the green arrow on the map showing your position, it is a light seen through the fog that serves as your beacon (fig. 12).

Checking to determine that you cannot draw a gun, you feel much safer about what could come out of the water (you're still in a survival horror). Finally, nothing happens on the lake. You only have to press the forward directional button, and the left or right ones to go in that direction (this is the case in normal action mode. In hard action mode, you have to paddle yourself by using the two analog sticks). My longest recorded "Boat Stage Time" lasted two minutes and 48 seconds, and I can easily imagine that this period was longer the first time I played *SH2*. Bad with regard to your final ranking, this time, however, gives birth to deep-seated feelings. Though you only have to try to steer your course toward the light on the opposed shore, you are, at the same time, enveloped by the fog, and you're also listening to the noise of your oars rhythmically cleaving through the water of your boat floating across the lake, and of the hollow rumbling drone. You can be, as I've been, moved by your real-time crossing. Along the way you are prompted to have sympathetic emotions for James, for whom the crossing is a wilderness time, since he has just killed Eddie and he is finally reaching the "special place" where Mary is supposed to wait for him. Confronting this sequence, one can't help but think about similar ones in *SH: Shattered Memories* and *SH3*.

You are again crossing Toluca Lake in the reimagining of the original *Silent Hill*. This time, the light guiding the way is the one at the Lighthouse where Harry is hoping to find Cheryl at last—indeed, at this stage, you'll receive a picture of your daughter sent by the police officer, Cybil, but it is a picture of an older Cheryl taken by the Portland Police Department. Since you're back in the nightmarish world, the lake is frozen. The more you run toward the final destination, the more the number of creatures coming to attack you grows. At one point, they're too many and they kill you. Recalling the beginning of *SH1*, the failure does not bring a "game over" but a short cut-scene leading back to the "real" world, making you fall into the water. From this moment on, seeing the action from a first-person perspective, you have to swim the rest of the way and can look down at the bottom of the lake to see statues representing important moments in your journey. In a rare moment, the movements of the Wii Remote and the nunchuk that map the movement of your arms as you swim forward are really effective. If you do not want to let Harry drown, you have to swim. The two or so minutes it takes you to get to the shore are just sublime.

In *SH3*, after Heather and Cartland have laid the dead body of Harry under a white bedsheet in his room, Cartland goes outside to wait for Heather. You are then alone and in a position to search the apartment, accompanied by a melancholic musical theme. This gameplay sequence only leads you to find the Stun Gun and two batteries in Heather's room, while serving as a transition between two cut-scenes, the next one in the car being, actually, the longest one of the game. Nothing takes place in terms of action, but much occurs with respect to emotions, namely the empathetic and sympathetic ones. The fact that you are left alone with Heather's dead father and that you're made to leave the apartment where she has lived causes you to feel as much grief *with* Heather as sadness *for* her. If you're caught up in the story, anticipating what kind of hell is waiting for Heather in Silent Hill but not knowing if she'll come back to her home (you need to get the UFO ending for this return), you might have a lump in your throat when you step outside.

Just before he points out the question of duration, Christophe Gans gives the example of another sequence of *SH2:*

> In Silent Hill, our perception is limited to the halo of the flashlight that one carries with one. One only sees two meters away. Beyond, there is the darkness and its cortege of frights. At one moment, the character enters a courtyard, rustling of echos, that one guesses is immense. My first reflex was to go round while hugging the walls. That took me endless time, and finally I came back to the door by which I had entered. I knew then that I had to move straight to the heart of the darkness, without knowing what I was going to find there. This was an appalling moment. I had to handle my fear. (Higuinen and Tesson 2002b, 31; my translation)

The moment to which the French filmmaker and hardcore gamer refers takes place in the courtyard of Toluca Prison. Like Gans and me (since I have resorted to the same strategy of running, not walking), you might go around the yard before plunging into the darkness . . . to find a scaffold with three ropes. At the moment you draw near it, you hear a horse galloping. Worried because the radio did not alert you to a monster's presence, you might still turn around to see if a dark rider of some sort is rushing at you. But the rider and the horse remain unseen. In front of the scaffold, there are three slots where you have to put the three Tablets you have gathered in the prison: Tablets of "The Gluttonous Pig," "The Seductress," and "The Oppressor" (those Tablets are in fact associated with the three open graves and epitaphs found later, that is, those of Eddie, Angela, and James). Then, at the moment you deposit the last Tablet, the loud scream of a dying man startles you. Climbing on the rostrum to claim what the three Tablets should have bought you, you discover nothing. As for me, I gave myself the willies because I fell down off the scaffold. The simple noise of my fall made me expect the worst, but nothing happened. After an inspection of the rostrum, you still find nothing. It is upon your retreat to the entrance, empty-handed and after having taking control of your fear, as Gans says, that you are rewarded with a Horseshoe. The courtyard sequence of *SH2* is a truly memorable scene. It conveys perfectly the gaming experience of the series. It also summarizes what survival horror and, more certainly, what survival terror games are all about.

To Face Your Fears

In "Playing with Ourselves: A Psychoanalytic Investigation of *Resident Evil* and *Silent Hill*," Marc C. Santos and Sarah E. White assert that "our gameplay [of *SH2*] becomes James' therapy; he is compelled to repeatedly confront the demons (literally manifested by deformed figures that stalk his every move) of his past and restore his irrevocable fractured subjectivity (and James' subjectivity is certainly irrevocable since the game's common ending is a cut-scene depicting his implied suicide" (2005, 75). This is also true for Cheryl in *SH: Shattered Memories* insofar as, in addition to the answers given to Dr. Kaufmann, you are the one incarnating her dad throughout her revealing therapy session. Although you might well and truly go and give support to the player characters during their journey through Silent Hill, in the end the psychological play is yours. *Silent Hill*, the series, is nothing more than a great playground. It is by all means fiendishly designed to scare you. Nevertheless, as I've said elsewhere (Perron 2005b), it is a playground where you play at frightening yourself.

Conclusion: An Endless Nightmare

> Survive, you must have the will
> This movie doesn't end the way we want all the time
> ...
> Now it's too late, too late for me
> This town will win
> Too late, too late for me
> This town will win
>
> —*Hometown from* SH3 *soundtrack*

In order to bring some light on the dark world of *Silent Hill,* I have chosen to concentrate on an analysis of the experiential route through the resort town. I'm inclined to think that such detailed critical inspection of the fiction, artifact, and gameplay emotions elicited by the games is the best way to show both the greatness and the importance of *Silent Hill.* Inasmuch as they present the main elements and set the core game mechanics that make the series what is, I've also given more attention to *SH1, SH2,* and *SH3. SH: Origins,* the prequel, *SH: Shattered Memories,* the reimagining of *SH1,* and *SH: Homecoming* follow the path mapped out by Team Silent, and so I did too. But consequently, I did not enter *the room.*

Getting In and Out Of the Room

Silent Hill 4: The Room might or might not have been originally intended to be related to Silent Hill; it is in any case part of the series now. It revolves around Henry Townshend, the player character, who finds himself trapped in his cursed apartment in South Ashfield Heights (which is incidentally not in Silent Hill). Townshend is compelled to explore mysterious portals, which lead to a disturbing alternate world, in order to uncover the reasons for his entrapment. *SH4: The Room*'s plot is linked to the story of Walter Sullivan (first heard of in one of *SH2*'s articles and tombstones) and the activities that have taken place at Silent Hill's orphanage. That being acknowledged, it is difficult not to emphasize the independence of its gameplay from the rest of the series, independence that explains why it ends up here at the outside edge. In fact, the first reaction to *SH4: The Room* has certainly something to do with the longing for the first and past experiences that Natasha Whiteman is talking about in "Homesick for Silent Hill: Modalities of Nostalgia in Fan Responses to *Silent Hill 4: The Room*" (2008). Beyond a doubt, *SH1*, *SH2*, and *SH3* have built an important fandom that felt a strong allegiance to the series. However, remarks Whiteman,

> This allegiance can be threatened when the texts that inspire fan devotion are taken in new directions. Enthusiasm and excitement surrounding new releases is frequently tempered by the voicing of loss, criticism, and disappointment, and in extreme circumstance, anger, which feed into the creation of websites, petitions, campaigns, and tirades left on bulletin board forums and discussion groups. (2008, 33)

Through her study of the posts on the high-profile unofficial fan site *Silent Hill Heaven*[1] and of a particular 2004 thread in the *SH4* forum (no longer available online), Whiteman reveals how the fans—the comments hold as well for many game reviewers—were calling for a gaming experience that would fit their horizon of expectations, for a "commonality which must hold the individual parts of the series together."[2] As *SH1*, *SH2*, and *SH3* were "referenced as being more authentic," "*Silent Hill 4* is read as failing to demonstrate sufficient elements of the universe. In contrast to an ideal version of *Silent Hill*, the changes are read as corrupting elements, destroying the '*Silent Hill* experience.' In each post a longing to return is tangible" (2008, 43). Nostalgia becomes an important artifact emotion. The ironic suggestion is too easy to make: this is *SH4*, which should have been called *SH: Shattered Memories*.

As a matter of fact, Team Silent's main objective regarding the design of *SH4: The Room* was too far from the aforementioned idea of commonality.

Akihiro Imamura, the subproducer, and Akira Yamaoka, the sound director, music composer, and producer, explain in their postmortem:

> We wanted to make sweeping changes from the past titles and give players something new and fresh to play. Of course, changing something that has already proved its worth is always a risk, but we wanted to see what we could accomplish. We took on the challenge of affecting change from angles—from the horror concept to the game's subsystems. (2005, 36)

On the one hand, it is difficult not to agree with them that it was a good idea to trap someone within his own apartment and to transform it from a "place of refuge and comfort" to a haunted and hostile space. On the other hand, the player character Henry Townshend is not really prevented from moving since he is always traveling to the alternate world. Since the apartment is the location to go back to for healing during the first part of the game, and since the only save point is an orange notebook on a desk in the living room, it asks for a great readjustment in your gameplay when the space becomes haunted. Suddenly, you have to manage threats upon your return home too. If you save while the haunting is in action and did not light a holy candle to remove its damaging effect, you are damned to eternally die when you "continue" your game session—and to curse the game system, eliciting a negative emotion also stuck between the artifact and the gameplay, that is, frustration.

The absence of the flashlight and the pocket radio couldn't go without great notice. These are the true trademark devices of *Silent Hill*. Without the small portable lamp, you cannot set the brightness level very low in *SH4: The Room* in order to really feel more alone in the dark, as was possible in the other games. Doing so will prevent you from seeing important details, especially in the first-person perspective the game offers for the first time in the series. For instance, when the portal in the bathroom was blocked, I was trapped and puzzled for a good moment given that I could not see the symbols around the hole in the laundry room and could not understand the association I needed to make between the Succubus Talisman and the four collected Placards in order to open the new portal. With the general environmental lighting, the visual style of the game becomes similar to the one of *Resident Evil*. The resemblance becomes even more marked with the introduction of a limited inventory of 10 slots accessed in real time, as opposed to the unlimited one the gamer was accustomed to. Like the item boxes found in various locations of *Resident Evil*'s Spencer Mansion, collected items must be stored in a chest located in the living room of the apartment. This forces Henry to go back and forth between the Otherworld and Room 302, a gameplay scheme totally different from the progression structure or level design of the other games.

The addition of the ghosts to the horde of enemies is interesting as it signals, in the line of the ambivalence introduced in *SH3*, the human nature beyond the monsters, though it removes the flesh presence these have. Following Imamura and Yamaoka's postmortem, although the horror of the ghost is deeply entrenched in the Japanese culture, the specter, "an indefatigable being that ceaselessly pursues the player . . . is a very frightening presence to all, regardless of the culture" (2005, 39). It's quite scary to see a ghost coming out of the walls, and you may have your share of gameplay fear. Yet, in comparison to those of *Fatal Frame* for example, the ghosts become merely an annoying presence since they can't be killed like Pyramid Head, the chief *Silent Hill* monster. Imamura and Yamaoka acknowledged the problem: "Ghosts were too obtrusive. . . . Players were irritated at constantly being on the run from them and as a result, were incapable of fully appreciating the beautiful rendered game environments" (2005, 40). Late in the game, when it is possible to stop them with Swords of Obedience, the option is still not that satisfactory: "The concept of invincible enemies wasn't a bad one, but in the case of the ghosts, we made them too strong. In the retail version, the ghosts become 'unstunned' in 3–10 seconds. If we could change it, we would make the stunned time between 15 and 60 seconds . . . to give the players some respite" (2005, 40). In comparison to *SH4: The Room*, the gamer respires quite a lot more in *SH: Shattered Memories*, which is free of monsters in the "real world," which allows him to appreciate the beautiful game environments.

It is likewise because of fans' reactions to *The Room* that Konami listened to the negative feedback about the first version of *SH: Origins*. Since this first version was, according to the senior executive editor for *Electronic Gaming Monthly* Shane Bettenhausen, too close to "a *Resident Evil 4*–inspired look and feel," the project was rebooted. The revamped *SH: Origins* that we know today "wisely plays safe, closely mimicking the presentation and gameplay styles of fan favorite *Silent Hill 2*" with a few new touches, such as the breakable weapons (2007b, 77). Fans are more willing to accept changes in *Silent Hill: The Arcade* (2007), the arcade being more suited to the rail shooter genre, and to mobile phone games with their hardware, performance, or memory limitations. However, and *SH: Homecoming* bears witness, it is not possible to wander from the straight and narrow when it comes to the traditional survival terror (sub)genre.

Tracing the Lines of the Incubus

As with many conspicuous successes of popular culture, *Silent Hill* has become a franchise, similar to *Alone in the Dark* and *Resident Evil.* The far-off past and present of the resort town have expanded to noninteractive territories. In Japan, there is the novelization of *SH1*, *SH2* (2006), and *SH3* (2007) by Sadamu Yamashita, and the digital manga *Silent Hill: Cage of Cradle* (2006) and *Silent Hill: Double under Dusk* (2007) by Hiroyuki Owaku (story) and Masahiro Ito (art). In North America, not to mention the animated comic *Silent Hill: The Hunger* available on PSP's *The Silent Hill Experience* (2006), IDW Publishing has published six comic books since 2004.[3]

Silent Hill: Dying Inside (story by Scott Ciencin) is the first "frightening new chapter to the lore of Silent Hill" (2004).[4] With a look that is quite different from the usual American comic style, the drawings arouse—here and in the other books as well—particular artifact emotions. It is attractive to see how Ben Templesmith (issues 1 and 2) uses lines, ink stains, dark contrasts, and foggy and blur effects to render the nightmarish 3-D universe of Silent Hill and how Aadi Salman (issues 3, 4, and 5) brings into play larger brushstrokes and harsh colors with the reddish ones predominant. Of course, the story evolves around a known premise: author and psychiatrist Troy Abernathy and his patient, film student Lynn DeAngelis, return to Silent Hill to confront (their) demons. They get to a place that is, says Lynn to Troy, "feeding on what's inside us. What's inside you" (issue 2, 16). A corresponding play of ratiocination and a drama of proof are initiated. Has Abernathy's wife, whom he meets reincarnated as a nurse with a scalpel stuck in her neck, really committed suicide? What is Lynn's trauma hiding? Who is the demon-child Christabella, what does she want, and what kind of relationship does she have with her sister, who is drawn back to Silent Hill? Withal, the confrontation between the two sisters does not come to a conclusion in this chapter and continues during *Silent Hill: Dead/Alive* by Scott Ciencin (story) and Nick Stakal (art) in 2006. This last story is also the one of actor Kenneth Carter, brought to the nightmarish town when his house comes to resemble the paintings he has on his walls. The paintings are those of Ike Isaacs, whom he meets during his journey. The painter is the main protagonist of *Silent Hill: Paint It Black* by Scott Ciencin (story) and Shaun Thomas (art), published the previous year. Owing to such links, you understand that if you cross places you already know (Lakeview Hotel, Brookhaven Hospital, or Pete's Bowl-O-Rama), encounter monsters you've seen before (Insane Cancers, Numb Bodies, Twin Victims, or Pyramid Heads), the comic books have indeed their own intertextuality and textuality too, much more abstract or narratively elliptical than that of the games.

The showy and less restrained universe of the comics is certainly not like the universe of the video game. Hence there is one significant difference to underline between the two worlds. At the very beginning of *Silent Hill: Dying Inside,* Troy Abernathy uses his standing to sleep with one of his admirers. To say nothing about his nebulous relation with his wife, his intentions to take Lynn back to Silent Hill don't seem honorable. The book he has just published might well be entitled "You're in control!" but he is really not, nor are you in control of his behavior either. He overreacts to what he finds in town and utters many a "Fuck!" The quiet, lunatic patient bursts into rage and shouts, "Fucker! Gimme that" when she takes a gun from Troy's hand to shoot Christabella in the eye. Actually, as opposed to the quite composed Travis, Harry, James, Heather, Henry, or Alex, the protagonists of the comic books swear a lot. Consequently, they inspire more antipathy than anything else. It is difficult to feel fiction emotions such as empathy or sympathy for them, and this takes away from the feel of the videoludic experience. *Silent Hill: Sinner's Reward* (2008) remains, in my view, the exception to this pattern and the most interesting book of the group. It might not be a matter of chance, but it is modeled on the plot of *SH2*. With different tones and atmospheres used by the artist Steph Stamb, Tom Waltz brilliantly alternates between past, present, and future events to tell the story of hit man Jack Stanton. Jack is trying to start a new life with his lover, unfortunately the wife of his boss, who has no intention to let the lovers go away easily, even when the couple ends up in Silent Hill. For Jack, like James in *SH2,* the town represents his place of redemption. Jill, his sweetheart, is dressed like the nurse Lisa Garland once in the resort town and demonstrates the same sensibility. The monsters Jack meets prove to be past victims. Akin to Maria, Sara, the young woman he saves at one point and tries to protect later, is no different from the other creatures he has crossed. She pushes him to do to himself what he has done so many times before. The last pages are truly touching.

As judgmental as one can be about their fiction, comic books have their own language. The reader has to address not only the sequential continuity between the panels, but also the spatial montage of those panels. For instance, the layout plays a significant role in conveying meaning and in eliciting artifact emotions in *Silent Hill: Paint It Black* and *Silent Hill: Among the Damned* (2006) both by Scott Ciencin (story) and Shaun Thomas (art). However, relying on fixed images, comic books cannot reproduce the experiential flow of video games, as a movie can do.

Filming the Game

With a long section of the third chapter displaying the cinematic experience offered by the series, that there is a *Silent Hill* film (2006) goes almost without saying, especially since the video game has become, in recent years, a new source of material for films.[5] The French film director Christophe Gans—a hardcore gamer himself—talked about *Silent Hill* in the press long before he got to adapt it to the silver screen. According to his comments quoted at the end of the fourth chapter, he holds both *SH2* and the series in high esteem. His philosophy goes in the opposite direction of the approach taken by Paul W. S. Anderson for the *Resident Evil* films or, worse, by Uwe Boll for *Alone in the Dark*.[6] For Gans, who had to convince Team Silent to grant him the rights, it was not simply a question of profiting from the game's popularity, to resort to its characters or setting or to be inspired by videoludic aesthetics. He adapted the original material with all the consideration it deserves. "For me," he says in an interview on the film's French website,

> a good game is exactly like opening a good book or listening to a good record. In fact, no matter the support, it is only the quality of the emotion that counts. My work as a film director simply consists of finding the most effective and the most respectful way of carrying this experience to a new medium—the cinema in this particular case. . . . [It is] more complex for *Silent Hill* in that all people who played this game have in a way visited Silent Hill and have fond and personal memories. (2006; my translation)[7]

For the purpose of the seventh art, plot elements from *SH1*, *SH3*, and *SH2* are brought into the foreground, as well as the characters' psychology. It is now a mother, Rose Da Silva (Radha Mitchell), who is going to walk through Silent Hill. Rose cannot accept the strange ache Sharon (and not Cheryl, played by Jodelle Ferland) is suffering from and that could confine her to a mental hospital. In spite of the protests from her husband, Christopher DaSilva (Sean Bean), and in order to find the answers to her worries, Rose drives Sharon to the ghost town, which seems to irresistibly attract the girl. While they penetrate this disturbing world, Sharon disappears and Rose goes off to search for her daughter. Alone most of the time, she meets few people, among whom are Officer Cybil Bennett (Laurie Holden), Dahlia Gillespie (Deborah Kara Unger), and Christabella (Alice Krige), the leader of a religious cult. In his turn, Rose's husband is going to look for his wife and daughter accompanied by a nearby city policeman, Officer Thomas Gucci (Kim Coates). As in the games, the town of Silent Hill is going to deliver its terrifying secrets during the movie.

In *Les Cahiers du cinéma,* Gans talks about the movies inspired by the video game universe's spirit and asserts that *The Matrix* (Andy and Larry Wachowski, 1999) is the only one to have openly put its finger on the video game and to offer an accomplished project: "There is in *The Matrix* a will to represent a universe constituted, as in video games, of layers into which one penetrates. We sink farther and farther into levels and forget where we come from" (Higuinen and Tesson 2002c, 16). His comment perfectly describes the multifaceted time and space structure of the *Silent Hill* movie. The real city of Silent Hill, the one of 30 years ago shown through flashbacks, as well as the foggy world of the day and the dark world of the night—all these represent layers into which the spectator sinks with Rose. But the movie's inclination to explain things more than one needs spoils the descent. Although it answers to narrative requirements, the segment with Rose's husband and the policeman, Gucci, draws too frank a line between the levels and the realities. The scene where Christopher and Rose cross each other in the schoolyard without being able to see each other, as well as the end of the movie, which definitively separates the father from his wife and daughter, sets the existence of a parallel world from which it is not possible to get out. The strength of *Silent Hill* was precisely to be more evasive on this subject.

Besides the use of the original game music of Akira Yamaoka (the movie executive producer), the fidelity to the artwork leads to a complete transposition of the beginning of *SH1* up to Harry's awakening (described in chapter 4) and of several other scenes. While certain shots during the sudden appearance of Alessa's silhouette on the road and during the first progression in the alley are almost exact reproductions of those of the game, Gans exploits the possibilities of a more dynamic cutting. If he reproduces the vertical panoramic view on the second crucified corpse at the end of the alley, he intensifies the horror thanks to a close-up of the bloodshot eyes of the crucified, which we discover is still alive. To translate the spirit of this ghost town, he shows Rose's arrival in town from the inside of a shop window, the back of a garage, and through an abandoned stroller. Then, to truly respect the framing and movements seen in the games, more than half of the shots of the movie are filmed by a crane. Combined with movable movie sets, this large trolley with a long projected arm at end of which the camera is attached permits the real camera to move as freely as the virtual game camera. Having understood that it was primarily a visit in the heart of the dark city the gamer had experienced, Gans joins Carol Spier (production designer known for her work with the Canadian film director David Cronenberg, among others, on his film *eXistenZ* in 1999) to reconstruct Silent Hill and faithfully re-create the aesthetics of the game. Shot outdoors in the streets of the city of Brantford, Ontario (the movie is a Canada-France coproduction), and in the studio to better control the fog, or having its images retouched afterward in the computer, the film is really close to the idea of what you would think of as a "real" Silent Hill. What's more, shot in part in high-definition video (by cinematographer Dan Laustsen), the darkness keeps its thickness without a film image too grainy.

Insofar as the source of pleasure is not the same for a gamer looking at the translation of the game world to the big screen and a spectator looking at a horror film,[8] it is the first segment of the movie that will certainly please the former because it captures the nature of his gameplay experience. Radha Mitchell, who plays Rose, learned, at her expense, what it implies to be in the shoes of a video game player character: "For the first few weeks [of shooting], I was just running and running and running. And then, there was some more running, followed by a bit more running. And then I was being attacked" (Helms 2006, 48). It is pleasantly entertaining to see Rose out of breath reaching the edge of an abyss at the end of a street, to see her use bus routes to find her way to Midwich Elementary School, to see her passing though the school courtyard to flee enemies or running into the restroom, framed as in the game and haunted by the tears of ghosts of a young girl. On the other hand, already in the seat of an observer with no ability to intervene, the gamer looks at a protagonist left with few alternatives to flight. To make the situation even worse, Rose is handcuffed for almost 20 minutes. To compensate for this absence of means of defense, the number of monsters met during the search for Sharon is largely reduced. Instead of roaming in the whole hospital, the Nurses are, for instance, grouped in a single corridor. Using very little of the white noise effects Rose's mobile phone could have emitted, the tension of the off-screen space is also lower. Without the fear of seeing the main protagonist being killed as often happens in the game (no repetitive "game over" here in the vein of a *Groundhog Day*—Harold Ramis, 1993), the experience is less terrifying. There is nothing like the games for this.

Indeed, it is the games one always needs to go back to when one talks about Silent Hill. As for the games, there could be multiple endings to this exploration of the resort town. Although this book has just one closure, this is not the closing stage of *Silent Hill*. You can always plunge back into the existing variations of this world of terrifying delusions. Above all, there is another game announced as I'm writing those final lines: *Silent Hill: Downpour* is scheduled to launch at the end of 2011. To our great pleasure, let's hope *Silent Hill*, the survival terror games, will be an endless nightmare.

The *Silent Hill* Franchise (1999–2009)

Video Games

Silent Hill (PSone). Konami / Konami (1999).
Silent Hill 2 (PS2 / PC). Konami / Konami (2001).
Silent Hill 2: Restless Dreams (Xbox). Konami / Konami (2003).
Silent Hill 3 (PS2 / PC). Konami / Konami (2003).
Silent Hill 4: The Room (PS2 / Xbox / PC). Konami / Konami (2004).
Silent Hill: Origins (PSP / PS2). Konami / Konami (2007).
Silent Hill: Homecoming (PS3 / Xbox 360 / PC). Double Helix Games / Konami (2008).
Silent Hill: Shattered Memories (Wii / PS2 / PSP). Climax Studios / Konami (2009).

Spin-off Games and Remakes

Silent Hill: Play Novel (Game Boy Advance–Japan). Konami / Konami (2001).
Silent Hill: The Arcade. Konami / Konami (2007).
Silent Hill: Orphan / Mobile (mobile phone). Gamefederation Studio / Konami (2007).
Silent Hill: Orphan 2 / Mobile 2 (mobile phone). Gamefederation Studio / Konami (2008).
Silent Hill: The Escape (iPod / iPhone). Konami / Konami (2009).

Supplements

Art of Silent Hill (DVD–Japan). Konami (2001).
Lost Memories. The Art and Music of Silent Hill (DVD–Japan). Konami (2003).
The Silent Hill Experience (PSP). Konami (2006).

Film

Silent Hill (Christophe Gans, 2006).

Novels

Silent Hill: The Novel by Sadamu Yamashita. Konami (2006).
Silent Hill 2: The Novel by Sadamu Yamashita. Konami (2006).
Silent Hill 3: The Novel by Sadamu Yamashita. Konami (2007).

Comic Books

Silent Hill: Dying Inside: story by Scott Ciencin, art by Ben Templesmith and Aadi Salman. IDW Publishing (2004).
Silent Hill: Among the Damned: story by Scott Ciencin, art by Shaun Thomas. IDW Publishing (2004).
Silent Hill: Paint It Black: story by Scott Ciencin, art by Shaun Thomas. IDW Publishing (2005).
Silent Hill: The Grinning Man: story by Scott Ciencin, art by Nick Stakal. IDW Publishing (2005).
Silent Hill: Dead/Alive: story by Scott Ciencin, art by Nick Stakal. IDW Publishing (2006).
Silent Hill: Sinner's Reward: story by Tom Waltz, art by Steph Stamb. IDW Publishing (2008).

Digital Manga—Japan

Silent Hill: Cage of Cradle: story by Hiroyuki Owaku, art by Masahiro Ito. Konami (2006).
Silent Hill: Double under Dusk: story by Hiroyuki Owaku, art by Masahiro Ito. Konami (2007).

Original Soundtracks

Silent Hill Original Soundtrack. Konami (1999).
Silent Hill 2 Original Soundtrack. Konami (2001).
Silent Hill 3 Original Soundtrack. Konami (2003).
Silent Hill 4: The Room Original Soundtrack. Konami (2004).
Silent Hill: Zer0 Original Soundtrack (Konami, 2008).
Silent Hill: Homecoming Soundtrack (Konami, 2008).
Silent Hill: Shattered Memories Soundtrack (Konami, 2009).

Notes

Introduction

1. I'll be referring to the title *Silent Hill* for the entire series, using abbreviations for each of the particular games.

2. Since the power within Heather will be revealed only later in *SH3*, we are induced to believe that she is, as the manual describes her, "just an ordinary girl."

3. Reviewers assert that "*Silent Hill 2* is more of a great experience than it is a great game, fun in a masochistic 'I need a bath' sense rather than in the usual butt-kickin' way" (Star Dingo 2001), or that "you may have noticed that I haven't really talked that much about the gameplay. And that's because *Silent Hill 2* is more of an experience than a game" (Jocky 2001). As I will demonstrate, I disagree with this view and prefer to point out that "it's not just a game," an assertion made about *SH1* by Broas (1999). It is more relevant to talk about the "gaming experience," as Bassanelli did: "*Silent Hill* is different [from *Resident Evil*]. The developers had the courage to reduce the importance of action and they created a deeper, more mature gaming experience built on silences and painful waiting" (Bassanelli 2001).

4. Team Silent is Akira Yamaoka (sound director of *SH1*, *SH2*, *SH3*, and *SH4: The Room*, producer of *SH3* and *SH4: The Room*, series music composer); Keiichiro Toyama (director of *SH1*); Masashi Tsuboyama (background designer, motion, story demo designer of *SH1*, director of *SH2*, art director and monster designer of *SH4: The Room*); Kazuhide Nakazawa (director of *SH3*); Suguru Murakoshi (drama director of *SH2*, director and scenario writer of *SH4: The Room*); Hiroyuki Owaku (event programmer of *SH1*, scenario writer of *SH2* and *SH3*, drama programmer of *SH2*, event programmer of *SH3*); Masahiro Ito (background designer of *SH1* and *SH3*, art director of *SH2* and *SH3*, monster designer of *SH1*, *SH2*, and *SH3*, modeling of *SH2* and *SH3*); Gozo Kitao (producer of *SH1*, executive producer of *SH2* and *SH3*); Akihiro Imamura (game system programmer of *SH1*, producer of *SH2*, subproducer of *SH4: The Room*); and Takayoshi Sato (character designer of *SH1* and *SH2*, CGI of *SH1* and *SH2*).

5. This study is based on the original PlayStation version of the games.

6. At the time, I did not record my playing session as I did for this study.

7. And when James gets the flashlight, we have a little surprise: a mannequin rises in a sound burst to restart the action.

8. I borrow this distinction from Hochberg and Brooks (1996, 380–81).

9. Grodal uses the term "novice"; however, I would argue that this term is misleading because it connotes inexperience, and even if the gamer is a newcomer to this particular game he may still be an experienced hardcore gamer; even if the gamer is hardcore, he is a newcomer in a new game he is just starting.

10. There are three endings for *SH: Origins,* five for *SH1,* five or six for *SH2* (depending on the edition and the platform), three for *SH3* (a first walkthrough will always lead to the "normal" ending), four for *SH4: The Room,* five for *SH: Homecoming,* and five for *SH: Shattered Memories.*

11. Just think about the "joke" endings. Do you really struggle through such challenges once again in *SH2* to get the "Dog" ending? Symptomatically, Birlew recommends in the official strategy guide: "Be sure to save your game first so that you can take up where you left off and get another ending if you want" (2001, 134).

12. The November 2003 issue of *GamePro Magazine* lists "The Scariest Games Ever" (Editors 2003). *SH3, SH1,* and *SH2* are respectively numbers 7, 6, and 5. The first two games on the list, *Half-Life* at number 2 and *Resident Evil* at number 1, are still at the top of the list when gamers discuss frightening games. The others in the list are *Sanitarium,* number 10, *Doom II: Hell on Earth,* number 9, *Alone in the Dark,* number 8, *Eternal Darkness: Sanity's Requiem,* number 4, and *Fatal Frame,* number 3. In the PS2 scariest games listed in the October 2004 issue of *PSM, SH2* is second and *SH3* third. *Fatal Frame 2: Crimson Butterfly* comes first. If such "Best of" are currently numerous on the web, the first three *Silent Hill* games virtually always figure on these lists.

13. For each monster, Birlew even gives the radio range in meters and the frequencies of the noise (2004, 18).

14. So well hidden that no reviewers referred to it. This system seems to be new to *SH3.*

15. "Authorship in electronic media is procedural. Procedural authorship means writing the rules by which the texts appear as well as writing the texts themselves. It means writing the rules for the interactor's involvement, that is, the conditions under which things will happen in response to the participant's actions. It means establishing the properties of the objects and potential objects in the virtual world and the formulas for how they will relate to one another. The procedural author creates not just a set of scenes but a world of narrative possibilities" (Murray 1997, 152–53).

16. The "Quick Save" of the PC version of *SH2* strikes me as contrary to the essence of trying to survive the horror. Take, for instance, this comment from a reviewer on *GameFAQS.com:* "An example that shows how unsafe I felt when playing this game during the night with the parents asleep is that I had a grand total of 750 saves! with 700 quick saves" (http://www.gamefaqs.com/computer/doswin/review/R47783.html). But still, *Alone in the Dark* (I-Motion & Infogrames/Interplay, 1992) had this feature right from the beginning.

17. "10 Star Ranking FAQ" can be found online at *GameFAQS.com.*

18. Arseeth uses, with good reason, the term "target" instead of "victim," which he finds too strong. Since the gamer is as much played as he plays, he always remains under the control of the game's master and/or rules.

Chapter 1

1. This label has indeed been questioned more than once. For instance, Laurie N.

Taylor prefers to talk about ludic-gothic games (2009, 46–61). Following Matthew Weise, we also have to acknowledge that "all survival horror games are horror games, but not all horror games are survival" (2009, 242).

2. Since I do not have a strong psychoanalytic penchant, I would not go as far as Jean-Sébastien Chauvin and define the experience as an onanistic one, comparing the controller to a "joy stick" (a joy nothing less than sadomasochistic in games such as *Silent Hill*). What's more, taking a sort of male chauvinistic perspective, Chauvin points out in an endnote that video game controllers "changed as years went by: the forms are less aggressive, more feminine, tending toward horizontality where the first *joystick* stood vertically" (2002, 40 n. 4; my translation).

3. As Steven Starker demonstrates very well in *Evil Influences: Crusades against the Mass Media* (1989), this is not new; novels, movies, comics, radio, television, and music videos have all gone through similar periods of denunciation.

4. The two other games were *DOOM* (id Software / id Software, 1993) and *Mortal Kombat* (Midway Games / Midway Games, 1992). See, for instance, Au 2002. This decision was reversed in June 2003. As for the 1993–94 Senate hearings, see Kent 2001, 466–80.

5. Using *Medal of Honor* (Dreamworks Interactive / Electronic Arts, 1999) and *Tetris* (Alexey Pazhitnov, 1985), The Brain & Vision Lab at the University of Rochester (http://www.bcs.rochester.edu/people/daphne/) found out that video game players (VGPs) outperform non-video game players (NVGPs) on the localization of an eccentric target among distractors and were better at an attentional blink task. See Chang 2003.

6. Using *Max Payne* (Remedy Entertainment / Gathering, 2001) and *Half-Life* (Valve Software / Sierra Entertainment, 1998) against spiders phobia, *Max Payne* and *Unreal Tournament* (Epic MegaGames / GT Interactive, 1999) for heights phobia, and *Unreal Tournament* for tight spaces phobia, the Cyberpsychology Laboratory of the University of Quebec in Outaouais (http://w3.uqo.ca/cyberpsy/en/index_en.htm) has shown that video games can help overcome those fears.

7. I'm revisiting remarks I made in Perron 2005b.

8. Cognitive engagement refers to Noël Carroll's curiosity theory of horror and the critique of Carroll's work by Mark Vorobej (1997). I'll come back to these theories in the next chapter.

9. Following Amossy's ideas, I have compared the film *Anaconda* (Luis Llosa, 1997) to a snakes-and-ladders game and designed a board to show how it worked (see Perron 2007).

10. Atari 2600's games and manuals can be found online at http://www.atariage.com.

11. For a general historical overview of horror games and the problems such an approach introduces, see Therrien 2009.

12. For the comment on *Haunted House* see http://www.atariprotos.com/2600/software/hauntedhouse/hauntedhouse.htm, and for *Halloween* http://www.videogamecritic.net/2600hl.htm #Halloween. Gregory D. George gives a different perspective (2001).

13. For example, even if "we get into the game," it is difficult to corroborate a comment like "If you are a horror movie lover, *Friday the 13th* [the NES game] offers some *serious* spooky atmosphere" (http://www.gamefaqs.com/console/nes/review/R26043.html; my emphasis).

14. Win Sical and Remi Delekta are referring to *Super Mario Bros.* (Nintendo/Nintendo, 1985) and *Pac-Man* (Namco/Midway, 1980), not to survival horror games.

15. One chapter of Daniel Ichbiah's book *La saga des jeux vidéo* (1997) is devoted to the making of *Alone in the Dark*.

16. A classical strategy to surprise the gamer: the monster literally appears, since it's not there if you search the end of the room before taking the notebook.

17. This paper is sadly not available online anymore (neither is *Joystick101.org* for that matter), not even with the Internet Archive Wayback Machine. It pinpoints many important features of the survival horror genre.

18. This happens just after the shape of Cheryl/Alessa is seen walking through the Antique Shop.

19. For Carroll, "The emotion of art-horror is not our absolutely primary aim in the consuming of horror fictions, even though it is a determining feature for identifying membership in the genre" (1990, 186). As we'll see in the next chapter, fear is a price we are willing to pay for the revelation of the narrative.

20. This would fit what Carroll calls "art-dread": "The uncanny event which tops off such stories causes a sense of unease and awe, perhaps a momentary anxiety and foreboding. These events are constructed to move the audience rhetorically to the point that one entertains the idea that unavowed, unknown, and perhaps concealed and inexplicable forces rule the universe" (1990, 42).

21. For an account of the perceptual and cognitive activity in the gameplay of survival horror games, see Perron 2006a.

Chapter 2

1. Rouse says: "It seems that the out-of-game sections of computer games are more user-unfriendly than almost any other solo experience medium. It seems likely that game designers may be thinking that they are movie directors and therefore want to create a movie theater-like experience, despite the extremely different nature of the medium with which they are working. . . . Unfortunately, the only interaction with the cut-scenes that many games include is the ability for the player to skip them entirely. This is essential, since many players will want to skip over the non-interactive sections of the game, as any playtesting session will reveal. Forcing players to watch cut-scenes is a totally unnecessary limitation no game should attempt to enforce. As I explained above, better than complete skipping, is to allow players to skip forward and back through cut-scenes as they desire, watching and rewatching them at their own speed" (2001, 222–23).

2. But you still have to be ready to quickly get control over your player character for the many boss fights, or the end of a discussion with Eddie in *SH2*.

3. Imamura also says in an interview: "In the beginning, when we were working on the original concepts and drawing the designs for *SH2*, our designers took a trip to the USA. We walked around a small town near San Francisco, gathered information and took photos. We wanted to recreate the feeling of small town USA" (Mackman 2001).

4. *SH: Origins* and *SH: Shattered Memories* from Climax are also a British take on this Japanese-filtered American horror.

5. Here's the entire text of the book found in a replay game of *SH2*: "The name comes from the legend of the people whose land was stolen from them. They call this place 'The Place of the Silenced Spirits.' By 'Spirits,' they meant not only their dead relatives, but also the spirits that they believed inhabited the trees, rocks and water around them. According

to legend, this was where the holiest ceremonies took place. But it was not the ancestors of those who now live in this town that first stole the land from these people. There were others who came before. In those days, this town went by another name. But that name is now hopelessly lost in the veils of time. All we know is that there was another name, and that for some reason the town was once abandoned by its residents."

6. More on the history of Silent Hill can be found in the "Lost Memories" appendix of the Japanese version of *Silent Hill 3 Strategy Guide*. This guidebook gives an overall view of the first three games, including creator's comments and interpretations of symbols, events, characters, and monsters. An unofficial English translation is available online at http://www.translatedmemories.com/book.html.

7. If Christophe Gans's film changes this to fallen ashes, *SH: Shattered Memories* sticks to this principle since the city is covered with snow and the Otherworld is depicted as a frozen world.

8. From the script and guide of episode 13, online at http://www.glastonberrygrove.net/texts/script13.html and http://www.2000revue.com/tp/article.cfm?articleID=29 .

9. http://silenthill.wikia.com/wiki/Silent_Hill_Wiki.

10. Dan Birlew (aka President Evil)'s plot guides to *SH1* and *SH2* online at http://db.gamefaqs.com/console/psx/file/silent_hill_plot.txt and http://www.gamefaqs.com/ps2/437029-silent-hill-2/faqs/14102; Duncan Bunce (aka The Hellbound Heart)'s analysis of *SH3* and *SH4: The Room* online at http://db.gamefaqs.com/console/ps2/file/silent_hill_3_plot.txt and http://www.gamefaqs.com/ps2/919554-silent-hill-4-the-room/faqs/32557; CVXFREAK and Orca782's plot analysis of *Silent Hill* online at http://db.gamefaqs.com/console/psx/file/silent_hill_plot_a.txt. There is also the plot analysis of *SH: 0rigins* by ChildofValhalla and TheSnake online at http://www.gamefaqs.com/ps2/944634-silent-hill-origins/faqs/50918.

11. These are from a browse session in the late Silent Hill Forum (http://www.silenthillforum.co.uk/).

12. Ito also explained in the making of *SH2*: "My basic idea in creating the monsters of *Silent Hill 2* was to give them a human aspect. In the beginning, the game player would believe they were human. Then I proceeded to undermine this human aspect, by giving weird movements to these creatures and by using improbable angles for their bodies based on the mannerisms and movements of drunk people or the tentative walk of very young children" (Beuglet 2001).

13. Before the beginning of *SH2*, James has experienced prolonged hospital visits in order to be with Mary. In *SH3*, the action is still dependent on the past of a sick little girl kept alive in a hospital.

14. A theory supported by Duncan Bunce: "It is a question of perception, images being manifested dependent on emotional and moral viewpoints at the time that are inherent to a person. Heather's experiences and monsters are very much Freudian to begin with, based from her subconscious Alessa identity. We can never be certain what anybody actually sees, as each person is not neutral or devoid of humanistic qualities such as emotions which influence perception and face value judgment!" (http://db.gamefaqs.com/console/ps2/file/silent_hill_3_plot.txt).

15. This leads to the Bad Ending where Travis changes into the Butcher, a monstrous being and one of the bosses who is killing Nurses—therefore women—with a large meat cleaver.

16. There are four more endings: "Good+," "Bad+," "Bad," and "UFO."

17. See the entry "Samael" of the Jewish Encyclopedia, online at http://www.jewishencyclopedia.com/view.jsp?artid=106&letter=S.

18. Carroll (1988, 170–81) develops a model of narration based on a question/answer structure. The concept of "erotetic narration" can be very useful to explain the activity of the gamer at the plot level of the games (see Perron 2005a and 2006a).

19. See, for instance, Grodal's chapter "Cognitive Identification and Empathy" (1997, 81–105).

20. I'm paraphrasing a distinction made by Alex Neil (1996, 175).

21. I'm extrapolating this remark from Geoff King's study of mainstream action movies and the *Die Hard* video games (in King and Krzywinska 2002, 51).

22. On the other hand, Rouse is opposed to strong player characters: "But the player's character should be sufficiently amorphous and unformed that the player can think of that character in whatever way he sees fit. And fear not, after spending forty or more hours with that character, the player will come up with his own ideas of what motivates and drives his game-world surrogate. The character he creates in his mind will be one whom he likes and with whom he will want to continue to play" (2001, 230).

23. Shyamalan's movie plays fair regarding Cole's sixth sense, fair since it is strewn with clues. Mainly, the color red is always present in the image when the worlds of the living and the dead meet; temperatures drop when ghosts are present. Depending if and when the spectator guesses the trick, the story takes another dimension. Seeing the film again, it is possible to reflect on the real question of the film and grasp how the secret was at the same time concealed and revealed. But then, it is also obvious that the film cheats on Crowe's condition. Even though Cole tells Crowe that he sees dead people that only see what they want and do not know they are dead, the scenes with the psychologist are subtly edited to cut out the moments Crowe's actions would have led to questions about his condition. For instance: How did he get in Cole's apartment to sit with his mom and wait for him? Didn't he pay for his ticket when he got on the bus with Cole? If he is Cole's psychologist, why doesn't he say anything when the doctor suspects Cole's mother was violent with his kids?

24. For a better glimpse and more of this scene, see the clip titled *FUKURO* in the "Art of Silent Hill" section of the *Lost Memories* DVD.

Chapter 3

1. It will be shown in the next chapter that one of the objectives of the survival horror genre is precisely to make you lose control.

2. As a matter of fact, Morreal derives the notion from Eaton. Both articles are cited by Carroll, who questions for that reason the notion of control (1990, 245 n. 50).

3. I'm using the definition of intertextuality given by Gardies and Bessalel (1992).

4. Mostly web reviews, I must say.

5. But apart from the fog, King's *The Mist* is, with its huge insects resulting from Project Arrowhead, closer to *Resident Evil* than *Silent Hill*.

6. To quote Gunning yet again: "Rather than being an involvement with narrative action or empathy with character psychology, the cinema of attractions solicits a highly conscious awareness of the film image engaging the viewer's curiosity. The spectator

does not get lost in a fictional world and its drama, but remains aware of the act of looking, the excitement of curiosity and fulfillment" (1995, 121).

7. To quote Yamaoka at the time of the release of the game: "Apologies to the Dolby Labs 5.1 sound system, because we created our own." See http:/www.silenthillheaven.com/Site/SH3/txt/preview_techtv.html.

8. Unfortunately, neither Heather nor Alex explores the misty streets of Silent Hill to a great extent. They walk through, respectively, the indoor locations of a nameless town and the hometown of Shepherd's Glen.

9. As fans have found, many of the authors mentioned have also written novels that revolve around towns in danger. Jon Saul's *Punish the Sinners* (1978) and Jonathan Carroll's *Land of Laughs* (1980) can be added to this list.

10. Fan sites obviously take a great pleasure in listing such references in *Silent Hill*. See, for instance, http://www.angelfire.com/ok3/silenthill/rumors.html or http://silent_hill6.tripod.com/id7.html.

11. "Almost" because the pursuit of realism isn't over yet.

12. The search view's direction can be controlled in *SH2* by using the right analog stick. By pressing the left analog stick, one may activate a zoom device that has been added to *SH3*.

13. See Gwilym Wogan's review online at http://www.soundtrackcentral.com/cds/silenthill_ost.htm.

14. Yamaoka was asked in an interview: "We have heard that you created over 200 footstep-sounds for *Silent Hill 2*. Is that true?! If so, it is certainly very impressive!" He answered: "Yes, it is true. As you know, also in regards to creation of the sound effects, just like the music, I wanted to differentiate it from that which you hear in other software. I wanted it to sound more natural and more realistic than ever. Although it was a video game, I wanted to make it so that you would feel as if you were watching a movie of high interactivity. That goal was not limited to the music only, so I spent a lot of time in the sound-creation of footsteps and other sound effects as well" (Kalabakov 2002).

15. See http://www.konami.com/games/shsm/.

Chapter 4

1. The assertion has been made in the introduction of *The Video Game Theory Reader* (Wolf and Perron 2003, 8).

2. Actually, the notion of action tendency comes from the works of N. H. Frijda.

3. It is precisely this grisly metaphor that has triggered my analysis of the question of embodiment in the survival horror genre (see Perron 2009).

4. See, for instance, Lahti 2003.

5. There is even a "beginner action level" in *SH2* that allows you to "enjoy the storyline, drama and puzzles of *Silent Hill 2* without fighting" (instruction manual).

6. Contrary to Jonathan Frome (2006), I do refer to gameplay and not game emotions. As I have said before (2005a), the last expression would underline a production coming from the game itself. It would not put the emphasis on the personal experience of the gamer. As it is not possible to pretend to understand what is happening while facing a game puzzle (compared to the action of a movie, which will go on anyway), it is even more difficult from a procedural authorship perspective to be certain that the

gamer will feel a specific emotion. Based on his past experience and his actual performance, a particular moment will be more or less scary.

7. This is obviously the case for the gamer who does not know anything other than the information in the instruction manual and who does not read reviews—or a book—spoiling those beginnings.

8. Eitzen shows that the curiosity theory or the narrative-as-problem-solving theory is not enough to explain laughter in comedy. Emotion responses have to be taken into account.

9. I'm borrowing a passage here from Perron 2004. I've developed the ins and outs of this "stone face" in Perron 2009.

10. Extradiegetic activity has to be distinguished from diegetic activity. As Wolf and Perron say: "Player activity is input by means of the user interface, and is limited and usually quantized by it as well. We could further divide player activity into two separate areas, diegetic activity (what the player's avatar does as a result of player activity) and extradiegetic activity (what the player is physically doing to achieve a certain result). The two should not be conflated, as the translation from one to the other can differ greatly. For example, some shooting games could move a gunsight about with a joystick and use a button to fire, while another could use a controller shaped like a handgun for the same input; the onscreen action could be the same, while the means of input vary. Likewise, the joystick is used to input a wide variety of on-screen actions, including steering, rotating a point of view, or choosing from a menu" (2003, 15). Andreas Gregersen and Torben Grodal (2009) mark the actual manipulation made by the gamer (what they call "primitive action or P-action") and its mapping to the virtual environment as different. For instance, the gamer only has to press the "X" button (P-action) on the PlayStation controller to attack and kill a monster with a melee weapon or a gun in *Silent Hill*.

11. A distinction borrowed from Janet Murray (1997, 130–34).

12. In reality, Ryan distinguishes four strategic forms of interactivity (internal/external and exploratory/ontological). Regarding the ontological mode, the decisions "are ontological in the sense that they determine which possible world, and consequently which story will develop from the situation in which the choice presents itself" (2001).

13. "Consistent with their common dictionary definitions, anxiety was assessed to reflect a nonspecific sense of uneasiness and uncertainty about what was occurring or was about to occur. Fright was thought to reflect a more direct response to specific threatening events. Upset was used to detect any negative experiential aspect of a subject's response" (Cantor, Ziemke, and Sparks 1984, 26). The "made-for-television" movie *Vampire* was used for the experiment. The degree of forewarning about upcoming scenes varied at three levels (none, vague, explicit).

14. "The *explicit* version of the introduction to this scene read: 'The architect searches for the vampire and finds a coffin, but instead of finding the vampire's body; he finds his wife's body. She awakens and tries to seduce him. He is almost swayed, but then remembers he must drive a stake through her heart. She snarls and tries to attack him with her fangs. At this point he hammers the stake into her heart with a thud as she screams wildly'" (Cantor, Ziemke, and Sparks 1984, 25).

15. I do not take it into consideration, but Duvall (2001) also suggests the nagging feeling that something was missed on the way can be detrimental.

Conclusion

1. http://silenthillheaven.com/.

2. I must admit, I was one of those.

3. A new four-issue has been published in 2010: *Silent Hill: Past Life* by Tom Waltz (story) and Menton Mathews III (art).

4. A comment made under the picture showing IDW and Konami's people (including Masahiro Ito, Akira Yamaoka, and Hiroyuki Owaku) at the end of the fifth and last issue of *Silent Hill: Dying Inside* (June 2004, 28). All the issues are available as animated chapters in the PSP's *Silent Hill Experience* (2006).

5. I'm borrowing elements here from my French review of the film (Perron 2006b).

6. Paul W. S. Anderson has written and coproduced four films inspired by the *Resident Evil* series. He has directed two of them. The films are *Resident Evil* (Anderson, 2002), *Resident Evil: Apocalypse* (Alexander Witt, 2004), *Resident Evil: Extinction* (Russell Mulcahy, 2007), and *Resident Evil: Afterlife* (Anderson, 2010). Known as a bad film director, Uwe Boll has made many films adapted from video games. He has directed *Alone in the Dark* (2005) and produced *Alone in the Dark 2* (Michael Roesch and Peter Scheerer, 2008).

7. http://www.silenthill-lefilm.com/gans.html.

8. The film viewer might be disappointed as well. The famous film reviewer Roger Ebert (not a great fan of video games) commented: "I had a nice conversation with seven or eight people coming down on the escalator after we all saw 'Silent Hill.' They wanted me to explain it to them. I said I didn't have a clue. They said, 'You're supposed to be a movie critic, aren't you?' I said, 'Supposed to be. But we work mostly with movies.' 'Yeah,' said the girl in the Harley t-shirt. 'I guess this was like a video game that you like had to play in order to like understand the movie.' . . . The director, Christophe Gans, uses graphics and special effects and computers and grainy, scratchy film stock and surrealistic images and makes 'Silent Hill' look more like an experimental art film than a horror film—except for the horror, of course" (2006).

Glossary

artifact emotion: An emotion that arises from concerns related to the artifact, as well as stimulus characteristics based on those concerns.

boss: A boss is bigger, smarter, and harder to kill than other enemies or monsters. It is normally met at the end of level and has to be defeated to pursue the journey.

cut-scene: A cinematic noninteractive sequence that punctuates the game at key moments and that generally serves to advance the narrative.

diegesis (diegetic/nondiegetic): The world in which a story takes place, made up of everything that the characters who live in that world can experience. For example, the music played by musicians appearing in a film is said to be diegetic, and can be heard by the other characters in the film, while the film's soundtrack and credits, which the audience sees and hears but the characters cannot, is said to be nondiegetic.

Easter egg: A hidden feature (textual, fixed image, animation, sound, or game) discovered through specific and often unusual actions.

fiction emotion: An emotion rooted in the fictional world with the concerns addressed by that world.

first-person perspective: A perspective that shows the game world as if seen through the eyes of the player character.

gameplay emotions: Emotions that arise from the actions of the gamer in the game world and the reaction of this game world to those actions.

in media res: A narrative technique in which the story starts at the heart of the plot, rather than at its beginning.

nonplayer character: A game world character that is not controlled by the gamer.

player character: The main character of the game whose point of view and body are those of the gamer when he or she plays.

prerendered sequence: A sequence that is not rendered in real time, so it can display a higher resolution.

remediation (hypermediacy/immediacy): The formal logic by which new media refashions prior media forms. It is coupled with two other terms: "hypermediacy" (a style of visual representation whose goal is to remind the viewer of the medium) and "immediacy" (a style of visual representation whose goal is to make the viewer forget the presence of the medium and believe that he is in the presence of the objects of representation).

RPG (role-playing game): A story-based game where the gamer creates his character and chooses the specific role he wants to play. His actions and decisions will change and increase the competence and/or aspect of his character, as well as the course of the story.

shot: In film, a continuous series of images resulting from a single run of the camera. The action in a shot is uninterrupted. Shots may vary in length, have different sizes or scales, be fixed or mobile, defined by different angle, or show different depths of field.

shot/countershot: In a filmed conversation, two shots edited together in order to show the two characters in alternation.

third-person perspective: The perspective shows the game world as if seen through the eye of a virtual camera, showing the player character in the scene.

unlockable elements: Various elements (clothes, weapons) that are made available after the gamer has finished the game once, or earned through various achievements (collecting specific number of items, completing a mission by a specific deadline, killing a specific number of monsters, doing a series of specific actions, etc.).

walkthrough: Step-by-step instructions telling how to complete a game.

Bibliography and Ludography

Aarseth, Espen. 1997. *Cybertext: Perspectives on Ergodic Literature.* Baltimore: Johns Hopkins University Press.

Aarseth, Espen. 2003. "Playing Research: Methodological Approaches to Game Analysis." MelbourneDAC: Fifth International Digital Arts and Culture Conference. Online at http://www.cs.uu.nl/docs/vakken/vw/literature/02.GameApproaches2.pdf.

Amossy, Ruth. 1991. "L'industrialisation de la peur." In *Les Idées reçues: Sémiologie du stéréotype*, 121–42. Paris: Nathan.

Anderson, Lark. 2008. "Silent Hill: Homecoming Review." *Gamespot.com*, October 21. Online at http://www.gamespot.com/xbox360/adventure/silenthill5/review.html.

Au, Wagner James. 2002. "Playing Games with Free Speech. *Salon.com*. Online at http://www.salon.com/technology/feature/2002/05/06/games_as_speech/print.html.

Baird, Robert. 2000. "The Startle Effect: Implications for the Spectator Cognition and Media Theory." *Film Quarterly* 53, no. 3: 13–24.

Bartle, Richard. 2006. "Hearts, Clubs, Diamonds, Spades: Players Who Suit MUDs." In *The Game Design Reader: A Rules of Play Anthology,* ed. Katie Salen and Eric Zimmerman, 754–87. Cambridge: MIT Press. Also available online at http://www.mud.co.uk/richard/hcds.htm.

Bassanelli, Lorenzo (aka Harry). 2001. "Silent Hill 2 Review." *Ps2fantasy.com*, October 28. Online at http://www.ps2fantasy.com/files/silent_hill_2/reviews/50/.

Bateson, Gregory. 1972. "A Theory of Play and Fantasy." In *Steps to an Ecology of Mind*, 177–93. New York: Ballantine.

Bedigian, Louis (jkdmedia). 2001. "*Silent Hill 2.*" *Gamezone.com,* October 1. Online at http://ps2.gamezone.com/reviews/item/silent_hill_2_ps2_review.

Bénédict, Sébastien. 2002. "*Silent Hill 2*: De peur lente." *Cahiers du Cinéma*, special issue on video games, September, 56–58.

Bettenhausen, Shane. 2007a. "American Gothic." *Electronic Gaming Monthly*, October, 73–78.

Bettenhausen, Shane. 2007b. "*Silent Hill Origins:* Konami's Troubled PSP Prequel Back on Tracks." *Electronic Gaming Monthly*, October, 77.

Beuglet, Nicolas. 2001. *The Making of Silent Hill 2: Alchemists of Emotion.* Fun TV. 33 minutes.

Beuglet, Nicolas. 2003. *Silent Hill 3: Naissance d'une Renaissance.* WE Production / Konami. 26 minutes.
Birlew, Dan. 2001. *Silent Hill 2 Official Strategy Guide.* Indianapolis: Brady.
Birlew, Dan. 2004. *Silent Hill 3 Official Strategy Guide.* Indianapolis: Brady.
Bolter, Jay David, and Richard Grusin. 2002. *Remediation: Understanding New Media.* Cambridge: MIT Press.
Bordwell, David, and Kristin Thompson. 1990. *Film Art: An Introduction.* 3rd ed. New York: McGraw-Hill.
Broas, Andrew. 1999. "Silent Hill Review." *Gameassault.com.* Offline (last access date: May 5, 2003).
Cantor, Joanne, Dean Ziemke, and Glenn G. Sparks. 1984. "Effect of Forewarning on Emotional Responses to a Horror Film." *Journal of Broadcasting* 28, no. 1: 21–31.
Carr, Diane. 2006. "Space, Navigation and Affect." In *Computer Games: Text, Narrative and Play,* ed. Diane Carr, David Buckingham, Andrew Burn, and Gareth Schott, 59–71. Cambridge: Polity Press. Also online at *Game Studies* 3, no. 1, http://www.gamestudies.org/0301/carr/.
Carroll, Noël. 1988. "Narration: An Alternative Account of Movie Narration." In *Mystifying Movies: Fads & Fallacies in Contemporary Film Theory,* 170–81. New York: Columbia University Press.
Carroll, Noël. 1990. *The Philosophy of Horror, or, Paradoxes of the Heart.* New York: Routledge.
Carroll, Noël. 1999. "Film, Emotion, Genre." In *Passionate Views: Film, Cognition and Emotion,* ed. Gregory Smith and Carl Plantinga, 21–47. Baltimore: Johns Hopkins University Press.
Cavallaro, Dani. 2002. *The Gothic Vision: Three Centuries of Horror, Terror and Fear.* London: Continuum.
Chang, Alicia. 2003. "Study: Some Video Games Boost Perception." *Albuquerque Journal,* May 28. Online at http://www.abqjournal.com/scitech/apvideogames 05_28_03.htm.
Chauvin, Jean-Sébastien. 2002. "Du singulier au collectif." *Cahiers du Cinéma,* special issue on video games, September, 38–40.
Chion, Michel. 1994. *Audio-Vision: Sound on Screen.* Ed. and trans. Claudia Gorbman. New York: Columbia University Press.
Chion, Michel. 1995. *David Lynch.* Trans. Robert Julian. London: British Film Institute.
Crane, Jonathan Lake. 1994. *Terror and Everyday Life: Singular Moments in the History of Horror Film.* London: Sage.
CVG. 2001. "*Silent Hill 2.* Confirmed for Xbox Launch: Full Interview." *Computerand videogames.com,* May 23. Online at http://www.computerandvideogames.com/news/news_story.php?id=11567&domain=pn2.
Dansky, Richard. 2009. "Writing for Horror Games." In *Writing for Video Game Genres: From FPS to RPG,* ed. Wendy Despain, 113–26. Wellesley, MA: AK Peters.
Davison, John. 2001. "Fear Factor." *Official U.S. PlayStation Magazine,* October, 120–30.
Dika, Vera. 1990. *Games of Terror: Halloween, Friday the 13th, and the Films of the Stalker Cycle.* Rutherford, NY: Fairleigh Dickinson University Press.
Duvall, Hayden. 2001. "It's All in Your Mind: Visual Psychology and Perception in Game Design." *Gamasutra.com,* March 9. Online at http://www.gamasutra.com/view/feature/3097/its_all_in_your_mind_visual_.p.

Eaton, Marcia M. 1982. "A Strange Kind of Sadness." *Journal of Aesthetics and Art Criticism* 41, no. 1: 52–63.
Ebert, Roger. 1990. "*Jacob's Ladder.*" *Chicago Sun-Times,* February 11. Online at http://rogerebert.suntimes.com/apps/pbcs.dll/article?AID=/19901102/REVIEWS/11020301/1023.
Ebert, Roger. 2006. "*Silent Hill.*" *Chicago Sun-Times,* April 21. Online at http://rogerebert.suntimes.com/apps/pbcs.dll/article?AID=/20060420/REVIEWS/60421001/1023.
Editors. 2003. "The Scariest Games Ever." *GamePro Magazine,* November, 58 and 60.
Eisner, Lotte. 1973. *The Haunted Screen: Expressionism in the German Cinema and the Influence Max Reinhardt.* Berkeley and Los Angeles: University of California Press.
Eitzen, Dirk. 1999. "The Emotional Basis of Film Comedy." In *Passionate Views: Thinking about Film and Emotion,* ed. Gregory Smith and Carl Plantinga, 84–99. Baltimore: Johns Hopkins University Press.
Ekman, Inger, and Petri Lankoski. 2009. "Hair-raising Entertainment: Emotions, Sound, and Structure in *Silent Hill 2* and *Fatal Frame.*" In *Horror Video Games: Essays on the Fusion of Fear and Play,* ed. Bernard Perron, 181–99. Jefferson, NC: McFarland.
Freeland, Cynthia A. 2000. *The Naked and the Undead: Evil and the Appeal of Horror.* Boulder: Westview Press.
Frome, Jonathan. 2006. "Representation, Reality, and Emotions across Media." *Film Studies: An International Review* 8:12–25.
Gardies, André, and Jean Bessalel. 1992. *200 mots-clés de la théorie du cinéma.* Paris: Éditions du Cerf.
George, Gregory D. 2001. "History of Horror: A Primer of Horror Games for Your Atari." *Atari Times,* October 31. Online at http://www.ataritimes.com/article.php?showarticle=194.
Giles, Dennis. 1984. "The Conditions of Pleasure in Horror Cinema." In *Planks of Reason: Essays on the Horror Film,* ed. Barry Keith Grant, 38–54. Metuchen, NJ: Scarecrow Press.
Gregersen, Andreas, and Torben Grodal. 2009. "Embodiment and Interface." In *The Video Game Theory Reader 2,* ed. Bernard Perron and Mark J. P. Wolf, 65–83. New York: Routledge.
Grodal, Torben. 1997. *Moving Pictures: A New Theory of Film Genres, Feelings, and Cognition.* Oxford: Clarendon Press.
Grodal, Torben. 2000. "Video Games and the Pleasures of Control." In *Media Entertainment: The Psychology of Its Appeal,* ed. Dolf Zillman and Peter Vorderer, 197–213. Mahwah, NJ: Lawrence Erlbaum.
Grodal, Torben. 2003. "Stories for Eye, Ear, and Muscles: Video Games, Media, and Embodied Experiences." In *The Video Game Theory Reader,* ed. Mark J. P. Wolf and Bernard Perron, 129–55. New York: Routledge.
Grossman, Howard. 2007. *Silent Hill: Origins Official Strategy Guide.* Indianapolis: Brady.
Gunning, Tom. 1995. "An Aesthetic of Astonishment: Early Film and the (In)Credulous Spectator." In *Viewing Position: Ways of Seeing Film,* ed. Linda Williams, 114–33. New Brunswick, NJ: Rutgers University Press.
Helms, Michael. 2006. "Queen of the Hill." *Fangoria,* May, 46–49, 82.
Higuinen, Erwan, and Charles Tesson. 2002a. "Éditorial: Cinéphiles et Ludophiles." *Cahiers du Cinéma,* special issue on video games, September, 5.

Higuinen, Erwan, and Charles Tesson. 2002b. "Entretien. Christophe Gans: 'Ce n'est pas du cinéma!.'" *Cahiers du Cinéma*, special issue on video games, September, 29–37.

Higuinen, Erwan, and Charles Tesson. 2002c. "Christophe Gans: 'Les jeux vidéo ont remplacé la série B.'" *Cahiers du Cinéma*, February, 12–16.

Hochberg, Julian, and Virginia Brooks. 1996. "Movies in the Mind's Eye." In *Post-Theory: Reconstructing Film Studies*, ed. David Bordwell and Noël Carroll, 368–87. Madison: University of Wisconsin Press.

Hoffberg, Jonathan. 1997. "A Better Picture Through Sound." *Gamasutra.com*, August 1. Online at http://www.gamasutra.com/features/sound_and_music/080197/better_picture.htm.

Hudak, Chris. 2003. "*Silent Hill 3.*" *Gamesdomain.com*. Offline (last access date: July 14, 2003).

Huizinga, Johan. 1955. *Homo Ludens: A Study of the Play Element in Culture.* Boston: Beacon Press.

Ichbiah, Daniel. 1997. *La saga des jeux vidéo.* Paris: Éditions Générales First–Pocket.

Imamura, Akihiro, and Akira Yamaoka. 2005. "What's Inside the Room? The Horror of *Silent Hill 4* Investigated." *Game Developer Magazine*, March, 34–40.

Jenkins, Henry. 2004. "Game Design as Narrative Architecture." In *First Person: New Media as Story, Performance, and Game*, ed. Noah Wardrip-Fruin and Pat Harrigan, 118–30. Cambridge: MIT Press.

Jocky. 2001. "Silent Hill 2 Review." *Final-level.com*. Offline.

Kalabakov, Daniel. 2002. "Interview with Akira Yamaoka." *Spelmusik.cjb.net*, July 16. Online at http://www.spelmusik.net/intervjuer/akira_yamaoka_eng.html.

Katayev, Arnold. 2001. "Silent Hill 2." *PlayStation2Era.com*, May 10. Online at http://www.psera.com/scripts/reviews2/review.asp?revID=83&letter=S.

Keeling, Justin. 2001. "IGN PS2 Interviews Silent Hill 2 Producer Akihiro Imamura." *IGN.com*, March 28. Online at http://ps2.ign.com/articles/092/092865p1.html.

Kent, Steven L. 2001. *The Ultimate History of Video Games.* New York: Three Rivers Press.

King, Geoff, and Tanya Krzywinska, eds. 2002. *ScreenPlay: Cinema/Videogames/Interfaces.* London: Wallflower.

Kirkland, Ewan. 2007. "The Self-Reflexive Funhouse of *Silent Hill.*" *Convergence* 13, no. 4: 403–15.

Kirkland, Ewan. 2009. "Storytelling in Survival Horror Video Games." In *Horror Video Games: Essays on the Fusion of Fear and Play*, ed. Bernard Perron, 62–78. Jefferson, NC: McFarland.

Kirkland, Ewan. 2010. "Discursively Constructing the Art of Silent Hill." *Games and Culture* 5, no. 3: 314–28.

Krzywinska, Tanya. 2002. "Hands-on Horror." In *ScreenPlay: Cinema/Videogames/Interfaces*, ed. Geoff King and Tanya Krzywinska, 206–23. London: Wallflower.

Lahti, Martti. 2003. "As We Become Machines: Corporealized Pleasures in Video Games." In *The Video Game Theory Reader*, ed. Mark J. P. Wolf and Bernard Perron, 157–70. New York: Routledge.

Lankoski, Petri. 2005. "Building and Reconstructing Character: A Case Study of *Silent Hill 3.*" DIGRA 2005 International Conference, Simon Fraser University, Vancouver. Online at http://www.digra.org/dl/db/06278.03293.pdf.

Lovecraft, Howard Phillips. 1970. *The Tomb and Other Tales.* New York: Ballantine.
Lovecraft, Howard Phillips. 1973. *Supernatural Horror in Literature.* New York: Dover.
Luban, Pascal. 2001. "Turning a Linear Story into a Game: The Missing Link Between Fiction and Interactive Entertainment." *Gamasutra.com,* June 15. Online at http://www.gamasutra.com/view/feature/3066/turning_a_linear_story_into_a_.php?print=1.
Luban, Pascal. 2002. "Designing and Integrating Puzzles in Action-Adventure Games." *Gamasutra.com,* December 6. Online at http://www.gamasutra.com/view/feature/2917/designing_and_integrating_puzzles_.php?print=1.
Mackman, Paul. 2001. "Silent Hill 2 Interview: Game Producer Akihiro Imamura Tells All about the Making of Silent Hill 2." *Gamer.tv,* November 24. Online at http://web.archive.org/web/20031229223955/http://www.gamer.tv/page/feature/3924.htm.
Mactavish, Andrew. 2002. "Technological Pleasure: The Performance and Narrative of the Technology in *Half-Life* and Other High-Tech Computer Games." In *ScreenPlay: Cinema/Videogames/Interfaces,* ed. Geoff King and Tanya Krzywinska, 33–49. London: Wallflower.
Maragos, Nich. 2001. "GIA Staff Favorites for 2001. 4. *Silent Hill 2.*" *Gaming Intelligence Agency.* Online at http://www.psy-q.ch/mirrors/thegia/sites/www.thegia.com/features/f020104.html.
Morreal, John. 1985. "Enjoying Negative Emotions in Fiction." *Philosophy and Literature* 9, no. 1: 95–103.
Murray, Janet H. 1997. *Hamlet on the Holodeck: The Future of Narrative in Cyberspace.* New York: Free Press.
Neil, Alex. 1996. "Empathy and (Film) Fiction." In *Post-Theory: Reconstructing Film Studies,* ed. David Bordwell and Noël Carroll, 175–94. Madison: University of Wisconsin Press.
Perron, Bernard. 2003. "From Gamers to Players and Gameplayers. The Example of Interactive Movies." In *The Video Game Theory Reader,* ed. Mark J. P. Wolf and Bernard Perron, 237–58. New York: Routledge.
Perron, Bernard. 2004. "Sign of a Threat: The Effects of Warning Systems in Survival Horror Games." COSIGN 2004 Proceedings, Art Academy, University of Split, 132–41. Online at http://ludicine.ca/sites/ludicine.ca/files/Perron_Cosign_2004.pdf.
Perron, Bernard. 2005a. "A Cognitive Psychological Approach to Gameplay Emotions." DIGRA 2005 International Conference, Simon Fraser University, Vancouver. Online at http://www.digra.org/dl/db/06276.58345.pdf.
Perron, Bernard. 2005b. "Coming to Play at Frightening Yourself: Welcome to the World of Horror Games." Aesthetics of Play: A Conference on Computer Game Aesthetics, Bergen University. Online at http://www.aestheticsofplay.org/perron.php.
Perron, Bernard. 2006a. "The Heuristic Circle of Gameplay: The Case of Survival Horror." In *Gaming Realities: A Challenge of Digital Culture,* ed. M. Santorineos, 62–69. Athens: Fournos. Online at http://www.ludicine.ca/sites/ludicine.ca/files/Perron-Heuristic Circle of Gameplay-Mediaterra 2006.pdf.
Perron, Bernard. 2006b. "Quand le brouillard se dissipe: *Silent Hill, le film.*" *Ciné-Bulles* (Montreal) 24, no. 4: 42–47.
Perron, Bernard. 2007. "Anaconda, a Snakes and Ladders Game: Horror Film and the Notions of Stereotype, Fun and Play." *Journal of Moving Image Studies* 5, no. 1: 20–30.

Perron, Bernard. 2009. "The Survival Horror: The Extended Body Genre." In *Horror Video Games: Essays on the Fusion of Fear and Play*, ed. Bernard Perron, 121–43. Jefferson, NC: McFarland.

Perry, Douglass C. 2001a. "*Silent Hill 2*'s Producer Akihito Imamura Not So Silent." *IGN.com*, August 17. Online at http://ps2.ign.com/articles/097/097467p1.html.

Perry, Douglass C. 2001b. "Interview with *Silent Hill 2*'s Artist Takayoshi Sato." *IGN.com*, August 17. Online at http://ps2.ign.com/articles/097/097403p1.html?fromint=1.

Plantinga, Carl. 1995. "Movie Pleasures and the Spectator's Experience: Toward a Cognitive Approach." *Philosophy and Film* 2, no. 2: 3–19.

Poole, Steven. 2000. *Trigger Happy: The Inner Life of Video Games*. London: Fourth Estate.

Provezza, Bruno. 2006. "Interview Frederick Raynal." *Mad Movies*, special edition, April, 52–57.

Radcliffe, Ann. 1826. "On the Supernatural in Poetry." *New Monthly Magazine* 16, no. 1: 145–52. Online at http://www.litgothic.com/Texts/radcliffe_sup.pdf.

Ramsay, Randolph. 2008. "Silent Hill: Homecoming Banned in Australia." *Gamespot.com*, September 25. Online at http://www.gamespot.com/news/6198219.html?sid=6198219&part=rss&subj=6198219.

Riser, Michael (aka Quemaqua). 2003. "Silent Hill 3 Review." *Alloutgames.com*. Online at http://web.archive.org/web/20041026233217/ http://www.alloutgames.com/Reviews/silenthill3.html.

Rockett, Will H. 1988. *Devouring Whirlwind: Terror and Transcendence in the Cinema of Cruelty*. New York: Greenwood Press.

Roundell, Paul. 2001. "TGS 2001: *Silent Hill 2* Playtest." *Now.com*, March 31. Offline.

Rouse, Richard, III. 2001. *Game Design: Theory & Practice*. Plano, TX: Wordware.

Rouse, Richard, III. 2009. "Match Made in Hell: The Inevitable Success of the Horror Genre in Video Games." In *Horror Video Games: Essays on the Fusion of Fear and Play*, ed. Bernard Perron, 15–25. Jefferson, NC: McFarland.

Roux-Girard, Guillaume. 2010. "Listening to Fear: A Study of Sound in Horror Computer Games." In *Game Sound Technology and Player Interaction: Concepts and Developments*, ed. Mark Grimshaw, 192–212. Hershey, PA: IGI Global.

Ryan, Marie-Laure. 2001. "Beyond Myth and Metaphor—The Case of Narrative in Digital Media." *Game Studies* 1, no. 1. Online at http://www.gamestudies.org/0101/ryan/.

Sankey, Daragh. 2001. "Fear, Art and Silent Hill." *Joystick101.org*, June 1. Online at http://web.archive.org/web/20030512031856/http://www.joystick101.org/story/2001/5/26/17127/1497.

Santos, Marc C., and Sarah E. White. 2005. "Playing with Ourselves: A Psychoanalytic Investigation of *Resident Evil* and *Silent Hill*." In *Digital Gameplay: Essays on the Nexus of Game and Gamer*, ed. Nate Garrelts, 69–79. Jefferson, NC: McFarland.

Sato, Yukiyoshi Ike. 2001. "Q&A: Konami's Akihiro Imamura." *GameSpot.com*, March 4. Online at http://www.gamespot.com/news/2704392.html.

Sical, Wim, and Remi Delekta. 2003. "Survival Horror: Un nouveau genre." *Horror Games Magazine*, July–August, 12–16.

Star Dingo. 2001. "Silent Hill 2 Review." *Gamepro.com*, September 24. Online at http://www.gamepro.com/article/reviews/16877/silent-hill-2/.

Starker, Steven. 1989. *Evil Influences: Crusades against the Mass Media*. New Brunswick, NJ: Transaction Publishers.

Sterling, Jim. 2008. "How Survival Horror Evolved Itself into Extinction." *Destructoid.com,* December 8. Online at http://www.destructoid.com/how-survival-horror-evolved-itself-into-extinction-114022.phtml.

Tan, Ed S. 1996. *Emotion and the Structure of Narrative Film: Film as an Emotion Machine.* Mahwah, NJ: Lawrence Erlbaum.

Taylor, Laurie N. 2009. "Gothic Bloodlines in Survival Horror Gaming." In *Horror Video Games: Essays on the Fusion of Fear and Play,* ed. Bernard Perron, 46–61. Jefferson, NC: McFarland.

Therrien, Carl. 2009. "Games of Fear: A Multi-Faceted Historical Account of the Horror Genre in Video Games." In *Horror Video Games: Essays on the Fusion of Fear and Play,* ed. Bernard Perron, 26–45. Jefferson, NC: McFarland.

Thom, Randy. 1999. "Designing a Movie for Sound." *Filmsound.org.* Online at http://www.filmsound.org/articles/designing_for_sound.htm.

Tosca, Susana Pajares. 2003. "Reading *Resident Evil: Code Veronica X.*" MelbourneDAC: Fifth International Digital Arts and Culture Conference. Online at http://hypertext.rmit.edu.au/dac/papers/Tosca.pdf.

Vorobej, Mark. 1997. "Monsters and the Paradox of Horror." *Dialogue* 24: 219–49.

Weise, Matthew. 2009. "The Rules of Horror: Procedural Adaptation in *Clock Tower, Resident Evil,* and *Dead Rising.*" In *Horror Video Games: Essays on the Fusion of Fear and Play,* ed. Bernard Perron, 238–66. Jefferson, NC: McFarland.

Wells, Paul. 2002. *The Horror Genre: From Beelzebud to Blair Witch.* London: Wallflower.

Whiteman, Natasha. 2008. "Homesick for Silent Hill: Modalities of Nostalgia in Fan Responses to Silent Hill 4: The Room." In *Playing the Past: History and Nostalgia in Video Games,* ed. Zach Whalen and Laurie N. Taylor, 31–50. Nashville: Vanderbilt Press.

Wolf, Mark J. P., and Bernard Perron, eds. 2003. *The Video Game Theory Reader.* New York: Routledge.

Yu, Daniel S. (aka dsyu) 2002. "Exploring the Survival Horror Genre." *Joystick101.org,* March 18. Offline (last access date: April 26, 2003).

Ludography

The video game systems in parentheses indicate either the systems on which the games were released or the system on which they were played.

Adventure (Atari 2600). Atari / Atari, 1979.
Alone in the Dark (PC). I-Motion Inc. & Infogrames / Interplay, 1992.
Alone in the Dark: The New Nightmare (PC). Darkworks / Infogrames, 2001.
Castlevania (NES). Konami / Konami, 1987.
Clive Barker's Undying (PC). EALA / EA Games, 2001.
Clock Tower (PSone). Human Entertainment / ASCII Entertainment Software, 1997.
Clock Tower 3 (PS2). Capcom / Capcom, 2003.
Darkseed (PC). Cyberdreams / Cyberdreams, 1992.
Devil May Cry (PS2). Capcom / Capcom, 2001.
Dino Crisis (PSone). Capcom / Capcom, 1999.
DOOM (PC). id Software / id Software, 1993.

DOOM II: Hell on Earth (PC). id Software / id Software, 1994.
DOOM 3 (PC). id Software / Activision, 2004.
Eternal Darkness: Sanity's Requiem (GameCube). Silicon Knights / Nintendo, 2002.
Fatal Frame (PS2). Tecmo/ Tecmo, 2002.
Fatal Frame 2: Crimson Butterfly (PS2). Tecmo / Tecmo, 2003.
Fear Effect (PSone). Kronos Digital Entertainment / Eidos Interactive, 2000.
Grand Theft Auto 3 (PS2). Rockstar North / Rockstar Games, 2001.
Grand Theft Auto Vice City (PS2). Rockstar North / Rockstar Games, 2002.
Half-Life (PC). Valve Software / Sierra Entertainment, 1998.
Halloween (Atari 2600). Wizard Video / Atari, 1983.
Haunted House (Atari 2600). Atari / Atari, 1981.
Legacy of Kain: Soul Reaver (PSone). Eidos Interactive / Crystal Dynamics, 1999.
Max Payne (PC). Remedy Entertainment / Gathering, 2001.
Medal of Honor (PSone). Dreamworks Interactive / Electronic Arts, 1999.
Mortal Kombat (arcade). Midway Games / Midway Games, 1992.
Nosferatu. The Wrath of Malachi (PC). Idol Fx / iGames Publishing, 2003.
Onimusha: Warlords (PS2). Flagship / Capcom, 2001.
Overblood (PSone). River Hill Software / Electronic Arts, 1997.
Pac-Man (arcade). Namco / Midway, 1980.
Parasite Eve (PSone). Square Soft / Square Soft, 1998.
Parasite Eve II (PSone). Squaresoft / Squaresoft, 2000.
Phantasmagoria (PC). Sierra / Sierra, 1995.
Planescape Torment (PC). Black Isle Studios / Interplay, 1999.
Project Firestart (Commodore 64). Dynamix / Electronic Arts, 1989.
Realms of the Haunting (PC). Gremlin Interactive / Interplay, 1996.
Resident Evil (PSone). Capcom / Capcom, 1996.
Resident Evil 2 (PSone). Capcom / Capcom, 1998.
Resident Evil 3: Nemesis (PSone). Capcom / Capcom, 1999.
Resident Evil: Code Veronica X (PS2). Capcom / Capcom, 2001.
Resident Evil 4 (Gamecube). Capcom / Capcom, 2005.
Resident Evil 5 (PS3). Capcom / Capcom, 2009.
Rule of Rose (PS2). Punchline / SCEI, 2006.
Shadowgate (Commodore Amiga / PC). ICOM Simulation / Mindscape, 1987.
The Suffering (PS2). Surreal Software / Midway, 2004.
The Suffering: Ties That Bind (PS2). Surreal Software / Midway, 2005.
Super Mario Bros. (NES). Nintendo / Nintendo, 1985.
Sweet Home (NES). Capcom / Capcom, 1989.
Tetris. Alexey Pazhitnov, 1985.
The Texas Chainsaw Massacre (Atari 2600). Wizard Video / Atari, 1983.
Tom Clancy's Splinter Cell (Xbox). Ubisoft / Ubisoft, 2002.
Tomb Raider (PC). Eidos Interactive / Core Design, 1996.
Uninvited (Commodore Amiga / PC). ICOM Simulation / Mindscape, 1987.
Unreal Tournament (PC). Epic MegaGames / GT Interactive, 1999.

Index

Aarseth, Espen, 6–7
action tendency, 35, 96, 98, 145n2
Adventure, 16, 17, 19, 23, 27
agency, 8, 107–8, 114
Alien (film), 10, 114
Alone in the Dark (film), 132, 147n6
Alone in the Dark (game), 20–23, 24, 25, 26, 52, 67, 69, 80, 81, 106, 114, 130, 132, 140n12, 140n16, 142n15
Alone in the Dark: The New Nightmare, 28
Amossy, Ruth, 14–15, 16, 69, 141n9
art-horror, 29–30, 31, 42, 65, 66, 142n19
artifact emotion, 8, 65–67, 68, 76, 86, 93, 95, 98, 127, 130, 132, 149
Art of Silent Hill, The, 78
Asano, Minako, 77

Barlow, Sam, 51
Bartle, Richard, 6
Bassanelli, Lorenzo, 40, 56, 92, 139n3
Bateson, Gregory, 12, 13
boss, 5, 19, 30, 42, 43, 47, 49, 62, 63, 99, 105, 111, 131, 142n2, 143n15, 149

Cahiers du Cinéma, 96
camera angle, 1, 15, 21–22, 25, 78, 80, 81, 85, 86, 110, 115
camera movement, 1, 15, 25, 78–79, 81, 83–86, 98, 134
Carr, Diane, 33, 53, 90, 112
Carroll, Noël, 8, 16, 29–30, 41–45, 46, 53, 65, 66, 104, 107, 109, 111, 141n8, 142n19, 142n20, 144n18, 144n2
Castlevania, 26
Changeling, The, 75
Chion, Michel, 87, 91
cinema of attractions, 69, 144n6
Clock Tower, 7, 26
Clock Tower 3, 52, 110
comics. See *Silent Hill* comics
coping, 99, 109–11, 117, 119
cosmic fear, 30–31
curiosity theory, 8, 42, 45, 104, 141n8, 146n8
cut-scene, 6, 21, 25, 34, 35, 37, 48, 51, 58, 59, 62, 63, 77, 78–80, 84, 89, 92, 94, 100, 101, 102, 103, 107, 115, 123, 125, 142n1, 149

darkness, 18, 19, 27, 29, 37, 88, 115, 118, 124, 134
Dika, Vera, 14, 15–16
disgust, 8, 12, 13, 29, 35, 38, 42, 43, 45, 62, 65, 107
drama of proof, 45, 48, 51, 59, 130

Ebert, Roger, 55, 147n8
Ekman, Inger, 108
empathy (and nonempathetic emotion), 8, 12, 35, 38, 44, 53–54, 55, 60–61, 76, 123, 131, 144n3
endings, 4, 7, 55, 98, 100, 135, 143n15

Eraserhead, 68, 87
Eternal Darkness: Sanity's Requiem, 110
eXistenZ, 134
Exorcist, The, 1, 68, 70

Fatal Frame, 32, 52, 84, 129, 140n12
fear, 4, 12–13, 14, 20, 21, 26, 28–29, 32, 35, 42, 46, 53, 54, 59, 65–66, 69, 86, 88, 93, 107, 109–10, 118, 119, 129, 135, 141n6, 142n19
Fear Effect, 11
fiction emotion, 7, 8, 33–35, 52, 53, 59, 61, 67, 76, 78, 95, 97, 108, 131, 149
Final Fantasy: The Spirits Within, The, 77
fog, 27, 29, 37, 47, 55, 70, 71, 85, 88, 91, 122, 123, 130, 133, 134
forewarning, 88, 116–19, 146n13
Friday the 13th (film), 15
Friday the 13th (game), 18, 141n13

gameplay emotion, 8, 95–100, 126, 149
gameplayer (attitude of), 5–6
gamer (attitude of), 6–7
Gans, Christophe, 95, 121, 124, 132–34, 143n7, 147n8
German expressionism, 85–86
Grand Theft Auto, 6, 80
Grodal, Torben, 3, 8, 12, 98–99, 109–10, 113, 140n9, 146n10
Groundhog Day, 135

Halloween (film), 15
Halloween (game), 18, 20, 141n12
Haunted House, 17–18, 19, 20, 23, 141n12
horror (vs. terror), 31–32, 117
horror film, 8, 10, 13, 14, 15, 16, 34, 67, 70, 85, 89

identification, 53–54, 60, 108
Imamura, Akihiro, 16, 28, 39, 40, 43, 65, 79, 108, 109, 118, 128, 129, 139n4, 142n3
influences (of Team Silent), 68, 77, 78
inventory, 19, 22–23, 24–25, 26, 100, 101, 102, 103, 106, 112, 128–29
Ito, Masahiro, 38, 43, 53, 78, 130, 139n4, 143n12, 147n4

Jacob's Ladder, 54–55, 67, 68, 75–76, 77
Jenkins, Henry, 46

King, Stephen, 10, 28, 31, 68
Kirkland, Ewan, 46, 78, 92
Krzywinska, Tanya, 8, 34, 61

Lankoski, Petri, 97, 108
Lost Highway, 57, 68
Lost Memories: The Art & Music of Silent Hill, 76, 78
Lovecraft, Howard Phillips, 12, 14, 20, 23, 30–31, 56, 68
Lurking Horror, The, 26
Lynch, David, 39, 56, 57, 68, 87, 91

Making of Silent Hill 2: Alchemists of Emotion, 2, 35, 78, 143n12
map, 22, 24, 26, 29, 33, 61, 74, 81, 98, 100, 103, 106, 119–20, 121, 122
Matrix, The, 133
monster, 4–5, 6, 7, 8, 11, 13, 15, 19, 20, 21–22, 23, 26, 28, 29, 30, 32, 35, 42–46, 49, 50, 51, 54, 60, 63–64, 70, 78, 80, 81, 83, 84, 86, 88, 91, 92, 101, 102, 103, 104, 106, 107, 109–10, 111, 114, 115, 117, 118, 119, 120, 124, 129, 131, 134, 140n13, 142n16, 143n6, 143n12, 143n14
Mulholland Dr., 57
Murder of Roger Ackroyd, The, 61
Murray, Janet, 13, 17, 104, 107, 140n15, 146n11
music, 15, 18, 19, 21, 25, 78, 89–90, 133, 145n14

Nakazawa, Kazuhide, 81, 139n4
Night of the Living Dead, 1, 10

Ojina, Yukinori, 38
Onimusha: Warlords, 52
Overblood, 26
Owaku, Hiroyuki, 45, 51, 109, 130, 139n4, 147n4

Parasite Eve, 26, 52
Parasite Eve II, 100

player (attitude of), 6, 114
player character, 17, 19, 21, 24
play of ratiocination, 8, 45–46, 48, 51–52, 60, 61, 101, 104, 130
pocket radio, 3, 28, 88, 91, 92, 101, 117–18, 124, 128, 140n13
Poole, Steven, 11, 15, 24, 77, 97
primitive action (P-action), 146n10
Project Firestart, 18
Pyramid Head, 43, 63–64, 79, 81, 102, 120, 129, 131

Radcliffe, Ann, 31
remediation, 13, 21, 149
Resident Evil (film), 132, 147n6
Resident Evil (game), 1–2, 7, 11, 19, 23–26, 28, 29, 30, 40, 52, 67, 81, 89, 90, 92, 100, 105, 106, 114, 116, 117, 128, 130, 139n3, 140n12, 144n5
Resident Evil 2, 26, 81
Resident Evil 3: Nemesis, 8, 63
Resident Evil 4, 111, 129
Resident Evil 5, 111
Resident Evil: Code Veronica X, 95
Ringu, 10
Robinett, Warren, 16, 17
Rockett, Will, 31–32, 49–50
Romero, George A., 1, 10, 20, 26
Rouse, Richard, III, 10–11, 34, 45, 57, 142n1, 144n22
Roux-Girard, Guillaume, 87, 119
Rule of Rose, 52
Ryan, Marie-Laure, 113, 146n12

Santos, Marc C., 41, 125
Sato, Takayoshi, 54, 77, 139n4
save point, 19, 22, 24, 25, 93–94, 102, 103, 106, 121, 128, 140n11, 140n16
Scream, 15
Shadowgate, 26
Shining, The, 68, 74, 84–85
Silent Hill (comics), 130–32, 147n3
Silent Hill (film), 132–35, 147n8
Silent Hill (game), 1–2, 11, 26–32, 33, 37, 38, 43, 44, 55, 56, 59, 69, 70, 78, 79, 81, 83, 88–89, 90, 91, 92, 98, 99, 104–5, 108, 110, 111, 112, 115, 118, 119, 120, 127, 132, 133, 142n18, 143n10, 144n16
beginning of, 47–49, 77, 83, 100–101, 123
endings of, 4, 49, 50, 51, 140n10, 144n16
nonplayer character (NPC), 57–58
player character, 31, 52, 53, 54, 59, 97
Silent Hill 2, 28, 37, 38, 43, 44, 57, 59–64, 65, 68, 69, 70, 74, 75, 76, 79, 81, 83, 88, 90–91, 92, 93, 98, 101, 105, 106, 108, 109, 110, 112, 114, 117, 118, 120–23, 124–25, 127, 129, 131, 132, 139n3, 139n7, 140n16, 142n3, 142n5, 143n10, 143n12, 143n13, 145n12, 145n14
beginning of, 3, 59–60, 103–4
endings of, 55, 59, 63, 125, 140n11
nonplayer character (NPC), 6, 58, 62–63, 77
player character, 31, 52–53, 54, 97
Silent Hill 3, 28, 31, 37, 38, 42, 43, 44, 50, 59, 69, 72–74, 75, 76, 79, 80, 81, 88, 89, 90, 92, 93–94, 98, 102, 103, 105, 106, 109, 111, 112–13, 114, 115, 118, 121, 123–24, 127, 129, 132, 139n2, 143n10, 143n13, 145n8, 145n12, 145n5
beginning of, 50–51, 56, 101–2
ending of, 51, 56, 59, 112, 124, 140n10
nonplayer character (NPC), 58–59, 77
player character, 31, 52–53, 97
Silent Hill 4: The Room, 3, 70, 80, 87, 88, 93, 98, 106, 126–30, 140n10, 143n10
Silent Hill: The Arcade, 129
Silent Hill: Downpour, 135
Silent Hill Experience, The, 78, 127, 130
Silent Hill: Homecoming, 2, 11, 35, 37, 38, 43, 58, 69, 70, 72, 74, 76, 84, 90, 92, 93, 97, 98, 100, 105, 111, 112, 114, 129, 145n8
beginning of, 102–3
endings of, 64, 140n10
Silent Hill: Origins, 28, 38, 43, 48, 49, 51, 57, 58, 59, 60, 62, 70, 79, 81, 84, 90, 98, 112, 119, 121, 129, 142n4, 143n10, 143n15
beginning of, 46–47
endings of, 47, 140n10, 143n15
nonplayer character (NPC), 57–58
player character, 31, 52, 53, 54, 97
Silent Hill: Shattered Memories, 3, 28, 72,

Silent Hill: Shattered Memories (continued) 74, 77, 88, 97, 98, 106, 109, 112, 120, 121, 123, 125, 127, 129, 143n7
   ending, 93, 123, 140n10
Silent Hill: Origins Official Strategy Guide, 119
Silent Hill 2 Official Strategy Guide, 119, 140n11
Silent Hill 3: Naissance d'une Renaissance (Making of), 90
Silent Hill 3 Official Strategy Guide, 4, 40, 143n6
Silent Hill (resort town), 35–40, 48, 52, 74–75, 85, 114, 130, 142n3, 143n5
Sixth Sense, The, 61, 67, 144n23
sound, 17, 18, 21, 86, 87–92, 115–19
stalker film, 15
startle effect, 15, 88, 115–16
Sugawara, Sachiko, 77
Sweet Home (film), 18
Sweet Home (game), 18–20, 21, 23, 24, 25

Tan, Ed S., 7, 29, 34–35, 38, 53–54, 66–67, 96–97, 107
Team Silent, 3, 27, 29, 33, 54, 57, 68, 89, 114, 119, 120, 126, 127, 132, 139n4
Tender Loving Care, 93
terror (vs. horror), 31–32, 117
Texas Chainsaw Massacre, The (game), 20
third-person perspective (vs. first-person), 22, 149, 150
Tomb Raider, 84
Tosca, Susana Pajares, 95, 99
Toyama, Keiichiro, 81, 139n4
Toy Story, 68, 79
Tsuboyama, Masashi, 29, 37, 61, 81, 104, 120, 139n4
Twin Peaks, 39–40, 68, 89

Uninvited, 26

Vorobej, Mark, 13, 42, 44, 45, 46, 141n8

Weise, Matthew, 26, 141n1
White, Sarah E., 41, 125
Witheman, Natasha, 127

Yamaoka, Akira, 35, 38, 53, 87, 89–91, 128, 129, 133, 139n4, 145n7, 145n14, 147n4
Yuri, Shingo, 77